GETTING READY TO

LESLIE H. WOODSON

Other Books by Les Woodson:

A View from the Cornerstone
Divorce and the Gospel of Grace
Eight Days of Glory
Evangelism for Today's Church
Hell and Salvation
How to Get to Heaven without Being Good
Make My Day!
Population, Pollution, and Prophecy
Signs in the Son
The Beginning
The Church: United or Untied
The Swinging Church
What You Believe and Why

Packaged by WinePress Publishing, PO Box 428, Enumclaw, WA 98022. The views expressed or implied in this work do not necessarily reflect those of WinePress Publishing. Ultimate design, content, and editorial accuracy of this work are the responsibilities of the author(s).

Unless otherwise noted all scriptures are taken from the Holy Bible, King James Version.

ISBN 1-57921-286-7
Library of Congress Catalog Card Number: 00-100227

Contents

INTRODUCTION

Is there any question that trembles on the edge of our consciousness with more pressing urgency today than "What on earth is life all about?" Sometimes this question is asked openly and defiantly, but more often it just vibrates in the subconscious without ever becoming articulated. To be sure, our generation is not the first to be troubled by this question, though it may be more pronounced with us. The alarming increase in persons with emotional disorders, many of whom throw themselves away with utter abandonment like men and women without hope, bespeaks our deep confusion about objectives.

The number one problem of our modern world is meaninglessness. Many find themselves engaged in a life and death struggle to discover some reason for human life, a reason for its origin and its continuance. Masses of intelligent people have given up the search in cynical certainty that to look further is useless. For them, the universe has no rationale behind it. Everything is fated for man and what he does or does not do is of little consequence. Under the hopelessness of such a negative philosophy these people either commit suicide, glut their sensual appetites, withdraw from society, lose their sanity, or try to fake a smile in their drab and hateful world.

There are great numbers who have not become so adamant about this absence of meaning. They are just puzzled by it all. It seems that there should be a purpose somewhere, but they have not found it. True, they are skeptics. Yet, one could hardly call them cynics since there is lingering around their minds a willingness, maybe an anxiousness, to have their doubts erased. They are not the kind of folk who will allow the wool to be pulled over their eyes, however, for they are alert and quick to detect a phony. We refer, of course, to the younger generation of the modern world, those between the ages of thirteen and thirty. Some of them, to be sure, are using the contemporary confusion as a cover-up for doing their thing. Always, in every group, one can find examples of dishonesty. Many of these youths, whatever their elders say, are searching and we owe them the best answers we have.

That is exactly what this book is all about. In the pages that follow, we will attempt to uncover some answers. It is my candid opinion that answers can be found if we are willing to dig deeply enough in the debris of secular, intellectual, and technological abortions to find them. Some of the answers have been covered over for as long as the Law had been neglected in the refuse of the temple, when young Josiah came to the throne of Judah in the seventh century before Christ. And the results of our having buried the answers for so long may be as devastating for us as was that situation in Judah. When the Law was found, reform was initiated in the land, but the apostasy was too deep for Josiah's revival to save the nation (2 Kings 22). Only a faithful remnant was spared, but from that remnant came the Messiah.

For too many years to remember, it has been unscholarly to relate man's earthly life to another world. People who have dared to suggest that the life to come must be given serious consideration in this world have been called by that ugly name otherworldly. We are accused of dreaming about pie in the sky by and by. Ours is a secular age. Man has grown up now; he is no longer a child of God or the product of any other unnamed childish fantasy. This is the arena where it is happening, and there is nothing farther on to get excited about. If there should happen to be, it has nothing to do with who man is or where he is right now. Such has been the reasoning in our time, both in the world and in the church.

When religion becomes completely secular, totally committed to a this-worldly concept, it loses its distinctiveness. Such religion is only more of what man had without it. No one would suggest that dedicated service to this present world is to be denied or neglected. Christianity is a way of life deeply involved in service. But we must see reality with both eyes, not just one. Gregory the Great, of the sixth century, may be said to have been one of the few ecclesiastical leaders who looked at life with both eyes. He was both an activist and a mystic. While admitting that most people will gravitate to the active life, he insisted that the best life on earth is that which is an anticipation of heaven itself. This contemplative life is what is missing in our world today, and the price we are paying for its absence is a loss of meaning.

Secular man has experimented with every known human answer to the riddle of life. Not one of his answers has met the need in the empty hearts of men, women, and young people in our time. This book is built on the premise that life can never have meaning unless it is consciously, deliberately, and unapologetically integrated around the Christian belief in a world beyond. That means that man is on the earth to prepare to live forever. Everything he does and is must be seen from that focal point. Nothing else makes any sense. And it is time that somebody said so with the same audacity as that which characterized the preaching of Jesus.

With a prayer that the Holy Spirit will use the thoughts that follow to guide despairing men and women into a life of meaningful radiance, this book is written.

Leslie H. Woodson

Getting Ready to Live

In the Beginning God

At first glance, it would appear that there are two contradictory stories of creation in Genesis, the opening
book of the Bible. In chapter 1, man is created on the sixth
day after everything else is in place. However, in chapter 2,
the order seems to be reversed. There, the animals appear
after man has made his entrance. In addition to this puzzle,
we are confronted with two accounts of the creation of man
himself, accounts that present conflicting details. This has
led some students of the Bible to insist that we have more
than one author of Genesis and that the first book of the
Old Testament is, therefore, a compilation of stories brought
together by an editor. Similar attempts have been made to
discredit the book of Isaiah as a prophetic unity written by
the eighth-century prophet. Thus, we hear of Deutero-
Isaiah, by which it is affirmed that only the first 39 chapters were written by Isaiah. The rest of the material is said
to be the work of an unknown prophet. Likewise it is commonly affirmed that the Torah (the first five books of the

Bible) constitute an amalgam of narratives contributed by as many as four writers or groups of writers referred to as J, E, P, and D. All of this is a subtle effort, under the guise of intellectual superiority, to reduce the divine record to a human mix of legends and, as a result, lessen the authority of the written Word of God.

If the Bible cannot be trusted as ultimate truth, the human race has absolutely no answer to the question that has haunted mankind since the beginning. The question is "What on earth is life all about?" The creation story is one, not two. Moses, under the inspiration of God, has used a literary technique employed by teachers until the present day. In the initial account of creation (Genesis 1:1-31), we are presented with an overview of the divine activity, a kind of introductory outline that gives the essential ingredients of the seven days. Then, in the following chapter (Genesis 2:1-25) Moses fills in the bare outline of the preceding chapter. It should be remembered that there were no chapter divisions in the original text. The divisions are artificial and break the flow of the story. What appears to be a second creation story is not that at all, but rather an expansion of the literary skeleton in the opening chapter of Genesis. We might understand the device better if chapter two is seen as the Arabic sub-headings under the Roman symbols that mark the major segments, a filling in of the skeleton with muscle, sinews, arteries, and flesh. From time immemorial, writers have used this method for instruction and clarification.

The question that concerns us at this point is how all this relates to the creation of man, the highest form of life and the masterpiece of the mind of God. The events of chapter 1 move upward through the seven days to the crowning work of the Lord of the universe in the appearance of man.

And here are the words of Scripture itself: "And God said, Let us make man in our image, after our likeness; and let them have dominion over the fish of the sea, and over the fowl of the air, and over the cattle, and over all the earth, and over every creeping thing, that creepeth upon the earth. So God created man in his own image, in the image of God created he him; male and female created he them" (Genesis 1:26-27). Here we have a pure and simple statement of fact, the Roman symbol "A". When we arrive at Arabic number "1" in chapter 2, verse 7, the writer provides us with additional information. These words constitute considerably more than the earlier bare disclosure of fact. They tell us how God went about the business of creating man. Roman symbol "A" tells us what God did, while Arabic numeral "1" enlightens us on how He did it.

Man's Threefold Nature

Man is not comprised of a combination of body and soul. This was an old Greek concept that insisted man's body is a nuisance and is discarded at death so his soul can be released to float around in the disembodied state of the Elysian Fields. The Bible does not portray us as dual beings of body and soul, as the Gnostics taught, but as a trinity of body, soul, and spirit. And it is the spirit that is akin to God rather than the soul. Christianity does not embrace the doctrine of the immortality of the soul. On the contrary, Jesus insisted on the resurrection of the body, the complete man.

Lest it should be wondered why the previous discourse is necessary, let it be understood that without the explanation given thus far, the following comments would be too much too soon. Should anyone find some of what has been said to be tedious and laborious, it should not be surprising that, in the search for truth, discipline is crucial and patience is demanded. If what has been said up till now has been properly absorbed, we are prepared to digest some exciting but much overlooked biblical truth.

While religious people have no trouble identifying the physical body, and are usually somewhat sure about the soul, there is real difficulty in knowing what to do with the spirit. Hardly ever do any of us attend a funeral celebration for a believer without being assured that, although the old body is beyond repair and destined for the ash heap, the soul of the departed has gone to heaven. Little if anything is ever said about the spirit unless it is casually mentioned as a synonym for the soul. The impression is left that either the soul and the spirit are one and the same or the spirit is so nebulous that we are better off to leave it alone. What is not recognized, however, is that it is the spirit of man that is akin to God and continues after the death of the body and soul, which, in turn, will be clothed with a new and immortal body at the resurrection of the just.

Now let us go back to the biblical account of man's creation in Genesis. "No man has seen God at any time" (John 4:12), because "God is a Spirit and they that worship him must worship him in spirit" (John 4:24). It is "His Spirit that bears witness with our spirit that we are the children of God" (Romans 8:16). Because God has no corporeal body, no one can see Him. He is pure Spirit. Spirit is greater than matter because spirit creates matter; matter does not create spirit. Therefore, when Moses tells us that God made man in His own image, His own likeness, it means that we were made as spirit first and then given a body and soul. This is what it means to be in the likeness of God. The image of God has nothing to do with what is fancied to be the physical and mental differences between man and the lower animals. It simply means that man was made as pure spirit, while the rest of the animal kingdom was not.

Incarnation

Traditionally, if any serious consideration is given to the genesis of the human race at all, most of us have envisioned Adam as a fully developed superior kind of man, with hands and feet, to which the Creator gave His spark of divine life later. The seventh verse of chapter 2 in Genesis is commonly brought up to prove this view. Only one problem surfaces with this argument. It just is not true! Even Michelangelo seems to have shared the erroneous idea when he pinpointed the moment of spiritual imparture with the Creator reaching down from the heavens and touching the fingertips of a fully developed macho Adam. The point that continuously is overlooked is that the Spirit or likeness of God did not come to a pre-formed physical body, but the body was created to house the spiritual Adam already in existence.

Someone may point out that Genesis 1:28 presents some troubling words. Those words read, "And God blessed them, and God said, Be fruitful, and multiply, and fill the earth, and, subdue it; and have dominion over the fish of the sea, and over the fowl of the air, and over every living thing that moveth upon the earth." What is thought to be a problem is that man is commissioned to reproduce as well as to supervise a material world when he was created as a spirit only. As has been suggested earlier, the initial narrative of creation is the overview of God's divine work. This command was to become a reality only when man received his physical body and soul, without which there could be no reproduction of the species or control of the newly created order of animal life. And this is why Jehovah formed for Adam a body, as recorded in the early verses of chapter 2, a body that would allow him to function in a material world as God predicted he would.

This fact needs to be enunciated again and again. If man were to live in a material world and supervise everything the Lord had made, it would be necessary that his spirit would live in a tangible life form conducive to earthly relationships. For this reason God gave man a body and soul, both of which, as a result of the human creatures' experiment with disobedience, would die. At that point, the spirit introduced into the Garden of Eden (Genesis 1:26-27) would return to be with God until, as explained by Jesus, the morning of the resurrection, when the image of God in man receives an incorruptible body suitable for life in the Creator's world to come.

As an aside, there is welcome light thrown on the divine human nature of Jesus, which grows out of this more intense understanding of man as body, soul, and spirit. When Jesus was born in Bethlehem as an infant son of the virgin Mary, the event was far from the beginning of the superlative Person whom we know as the Son of God. Paul, in his letter to the church at Philippi, waxes eloquent when discoursing on the humiliation and exaltation of Christ (Philippians 2:5-11). There, the apostle reminds us that He who "humbled himself and became obedient unto death" was the same as He "who being in the form of God thought it not robbery to be equal with God." The form of God means the true nature or character of the heavenly Father—what God really is. So Paul is here joining John and the writer of Hebrews in proclaiming the pre-existence of Christ Jesus (see John 1:1-14 and Hebrews 11:3).

It is always true that the spiritual precedes the material and is responsible for its existence. Hence, man was first created as spirit and afterward given a physical body animated by a soul. Likewise, Jesus Christ, who is God incarnate, was always God according to His real nature or form, which is Spirit. At Bethlehem, God took on the body of man in order to identify with us in the flesh and redeem us from eternal death. But Christ did not begin His existence at the birth event. Let no one misunderstand us to be saying that man has a pre-existent spirit prior to his conception. Such a view opens the door to all kinds of nonchristian ideas, the most readily observed example being the theory of reincarnation. Man's spirit is created by an act of God at the moment of conception, after which He begins to form a body for him. Our argument here is clear. The creating Spirit was responsible for the forming of Adam's body *and* the body of Jesus in the womb of the virgin. Spirit creates matter, not the other way around. The writer of Hebrews is emphatic about this: "Things which are seen were not made of things which do appear" (Hebrews 11:3). With this fact clearly instilled in our minds, we better understand the meaning of the virgin birth.

To refresh our minds, let us turn again to the seventh verse of the second chapter of Genesis: "And the Lord God formed man of the dust of the ground, and breathed into his nostrils the breath of life; and man became a living soul." It is quickly observed in these words that man has been created (see Genesis 1:26-27) already and that now the Creator builds him a body out of existing matter ("dust of the ground"). Theologically, we are on a firm foundation when it is stated that God created man "out of nothing." The Hebrew word in Genesis 1:27, translated in the KJV as "created" means to make something from nothing. And that is exactly what Jehovah did when He made man's spirit! But when He made man's body, the Scripture plainly asserts that the physical part of Adam was formed from existing matter.

We can, with a little imagination, visualize the meticulous hands-on effort as God shapes a form for Adam's spirit until it is exactly what is needed to be the caretaker of Eden. But a body without life is a corpse. Therefore, we are informed that God took the limp form of man and blew breath into his lungs (the Hebrew word is translated *wind, breath, spirit*), much like the mouth-to-mouth resuscitation given today to one who is not breathing. This act was one of animation or the bringing of life to an otherwise empty corpse. The result was that "man became a living soul." And our confusion lies in the translation of the Hebrew word *nephish* as "soul" in the KJV. Of considerable importance is the fact that the same Hebrew word is used of the animals and translated as "creature." The point is that this is the moment when man became a conscious being like the animals. This distinguishes man and the animals from the plants that have unconscious life. In this sense, animals have souls too. So this is not the moment when man was made in God's image. That happened earlier when he was created out of nothing as pure spirit (look again at Genesis 1:27). All of this means that we do not believe in the immortality of the soul (there is nothing immortal about the soul), but we do believe in "the resurrection of the body and the life everlasting."

What Life Is All About

Everlasting life, however, was dependent on a required specific obedience insisted upon by the Creator Himself. Now we must read the word of the Lord which came to Adam after he caught his breath: "The Lord God commanded the man, saying, Of every tree of the garden thou mayest freely eat; but of the tree of the knowledge of good and evil, thou shalt not eat of it; for in the day that thou eatest thereof thou shalt surely die" (Genesis 2:15-17). The question this book asks is what on earth is life all about? Surely, no one can miss the obvious fact that being here entails responsibility of mammoth proportions. Our business is twofold. First, we are to take care of the earth and everything the Creator has put here. Second, we are to prepare ourselves for the coming hour of accountability when we stand before the Judge of all the earth who will ask us, "What have you made of your life? Did you learn your lessons well? Are you ready for the *next* lesson?"

The first Adam handled his life and the awesome charge committed to him to his discredit. Disobedience carries a heavy punishment. The Creator stands over His world in judgment, but that judgment is always tempered with mercy. Although Adam and his helpmate were driven from the garden, they were not abandoned by God. From the outset, there was provision made that future sin would be covered by the system of sacrifice that Abel understood when he brought his lamb to the altar. There is little doubt that Adam had explained the divine command for blood sacrifice to his family on the very day God covered the shame of Adam's own naked sinfulness with the skin of a slain animal. None of us should entertain the mistaken notion that man was accepted by God, prior to the death of Christ, by keeping the Law. The Law was never intended to save anyone. We have from the beginning been saved by faith that takes God at His Word, which promises that our sins will be covered by blood sacrifice. Augustine was right when he reminded us that the Christian religion existed from the dawn of the human race and was only named Christian when Christ came in the flesh. Jehovah God has never altered His demands, nor has He changed the method by which forgiveness can be received when those divine expectations are unfulfilled.

At the precise moment the human race had developed into its relative maturity, God put an end to the temporary system of blood sacrifice by giving His Son as both the officiating Priest and the Sacrifice. By the crucifixion of Christ, the perfect and unblemished sacrifice, every one of us can now be forgiven and restored to the relationship with the Creator that Adam enjoyed prior to the Fall. What the first Adam lost for us, the last Adam has given back. And by repentance and faith in the death and resurrection of Jesus Christ, we can begin again.

At this point, we find the first hint at what on earth life is all about. And from this sunrise of purpose, each one of us is ushered into the early morning of a long day with all the joys and sorrows it may bring. It is from this climacteric second that the believer is forced to discover what life is all about. Of course, the man or woman, who never comes to know God through Christ, is destined to a lifetime of ignorance to the meaning of human existence.

As a result of conversion to Christ as Savior, our lives take on an entirely new meaning directly related to a change in our spiritual makeup. Prior to the new birth, man is "dead in trespasses and sins" (Ephesians 2:1). That is, the image of God in man lies dormant, not destroyed but totally defaced by the Fall. There is little spirit life in the unregenerate person. Often it is said of a vivacious, enthusiastic individual that he has a lot of spirit, but what we mean by that expression is that he gives evidence of a lot of soul, an

18

above average degree of vitality. At the moment of conception, although no one knows how it happens, the image of God is instantly alive and the process begins within the mother's womb by which the Creator, over the next nine months, forms a body and soul for the spirit. When the infant is born, it begins a journey of innocence characterized by a dormant spirit and an extremely energetic soul.

God's design from the beginning of creation was that the living spirit (the image of God in man) would not only reside in a body animated by a developing soul (*psyche*), but that the spirit would supervise and control the degenerative tendency of both soul and body. Without such spiritual control, man has little chance to do anything other than deteriorate as his ego-centered soul rules over a readily submissive body.

What man cannot do is properly control himself when his spirit is dead, a fact easily observed in every child when he arrives at the unspecified age of moral accountability. Prior to such a time, it is the parents or guardians who make the decisions not to eat poison berries from the bush, beat up on one's siblings, steal from the cookie jar, or break the neighbor's windows. Following this decisive moment of accountability one still needs to be continually pointed in the right direction, a task parents gradually relinquish as the "I-will-do-it-myself" attitude grows. The result is tragedy, unless Someone steps in to fill the role of "We-can do-no-more" fathers and mothers. And that is where the image of God takes over, but only when a young man or woman seeks a divine Director, who alone can restore that smoldering spark of spirit into a roaring flame. "When he, the Spirit of truth, is come, he will guide you into all truth" (John 16:13). Unless there is divine instruction, human life degenerates into chaos.

Spirit, Soul, and Body

To fully understand the impact of these words, it would be helpful to secure a blank sheet of paper and draw three concentric circles on it, circles of three diameters all having the same center. Label the inner circle *spirit*, the outer circle *body,* and the middle circle *soul*. Now mark a big "X" over the inner circle declaring the spirit dead. Write the five senses (sight, sound, smell, taste, and touch) within the middle circle.

What the body, represented by the outer circle, does with itself is dictated by how the senses affect the mind (soul). This is where we get into trouble, because the natural mind is carnal and, with a decadent spirit that is out of touch with God, continually inducing faulty action.

While the natural man cannot conceive of such a thing, the ideal arrangement is to have a renewal of the spirit so that the spirit controls the mind, which in turn directs the function of the body according to the will of God. This is what Christians mean when we talk about being *saved*. It is the rebirth of the spirit within that saves us from an uncontrolled and misdirected life whose destination is hell—here and hereafter.

Life is to be recognized as a testing ground for something farther on in our future. More will be said about this in later chapters. This rebirth of the spirit is what the Bible calls justification. And that which follows as the Holy Spirit shapes and disciplines the soul and body is what is meant by sanctification. It happens when the Spirit is given top billing and Christ becomes more than Savior; He becomes Lord.

Now we begin to see what on earth life is all about. Our three score years and ten are not an accident. Rather they are given to us by our Creator to prepare us for life in the world to come. How tragic it is to spend these fleeting years as if they were an end in themselves. Everything that happens to us is for a reason. Final triumph is not achieved by avoiding the hard stuff, but by meeting it head-on under the guidance of the Holy Spirit with the indestructible confidence that God is doing something with us that has a purpose.

As we look at the chaos and confusion everywhere across the world, the lack of moral values, the deterioration of long cherished institutions, the prostitution of religion, the lack of respect for human life, the constant threat of terrorism and war, and the general apathy of a world on the brink of insanity, we are apt to question the meaning of existence. Perhaps it is all just an accident out of the dim and distant past, a dream signifying nothing, much ado about something that makes no sense and is, therefore, of no consequence. The temptation to think like this is always present. Where we go wrong, however, is in looking at the wrong side of the tapestry. Turn it over and the design is right before our eyes no matter how we may have messed it up. The Creator has not given up on His masterpiece. We are on probation, but by the power of the indwelling Spirit our days and nights can become exciting and rewarding adventures in a pre-planned journey toward the Father's house.

It is we who must decide what shall become of us. No one else can make that decision for us. Some will choose to grovel in the dust without ever looking up. A few will choose to rise above that which clouds our vision and obscures the sun. We are told that ants are born with wings, that they experience the glory of flight, but then tear them off and deliberately live out their days as crawling insects rather than thrive in the vast empire of the air. And so it is with us. God has made us for Himself, even like Himself, with spiritual potential to overcome the chaotic world of evil preoccupation. He pursues us to renew our decadent spirits and give us clear perspective on the consummate goal of human existence as well as the means of achieving it. Yet, all the while we go about with our heads down, defeated by the unexpected things that happen to us, when lifting our eyes to the distant horizon would make all the difference in the world.

The Sense of It All

It will be the premise of this book that life makes sense, that absolutely nothing is left to chance, that "all things work together for good to them that love God" (Romans 8:28). There is no reason to believe that God created the world and then stepped back into the shadows to watch it run down. The Deists believed that, but they were wrong. Nor were the Stoics any nearer the truth in insisting that we must resign ourselves to fate without passion because what happens just happens. Then there were the Epicureans, who were sure that man's short stay here is so meaningless that he must get what he can while he can. Their philosophy was a bleak "Eat, drink, and be merry for tomorrow we die." Existentialists who live for the passing moment, as if life were an end in itself, miss the whole point. Earthly life is never an end in itself. It is a means to an end. And the end is resurrection and life eternal. Otherwise it would have been better never to have passed this way at all. To live and miss the purpose, is man's greatest tragedy.

Many people live their years like a rudderless ship with no thought as to where they are going. Some apparently do not care. The future is of little concern. Therefore, such men and women simply have no clue as to the whereabouts of the final port. Fearful of being accused of other-worldliness, even the church for which Christ died has a tendency to neglect anything that has to do with what happens to us after we die. This has not always been the case. In her saner times, the church has recognized that the distinctive mission given to her is the work of preparing us to live with God in the world to come. The shift in direction that the contemporary church has decided to make is unfortunate for us all. There are, of course, local congregations where the Gospel of personal redemption is still proclaimed. However, the general trend is a move in the direction of improving social conditions as if this were the only important consideration for today's world. By doing this, as good as the effort may be, the most pressing need of mankind is ignored and the only established institution charged with preparing men and women for eternity excuses itself by arguing that the thing that matters is the here and now. It all sounds like the pagan thinkers we earlier mentioned. And this is not a surprise when it is obvious that there is a rebirth of paganism all across the planet.

Regardless as to how improved conditions on earth become, we are all going to die. So what are we to do? Get ready to live forever! Could any objective be more important, more crucial to a fulfilled life? Even if someone could prove that there is nothing beyond the grave (perish the thought), there would be compelling justification for devoting every energy to preparing ourselves as if there were. That is an option which never disappoints one. After all, there is nothing to lose when we stretch for something better than this present world has to offer. The alternative is much too horrible to think about.

So much then for this old world. What are we to make of it? Where are we going? Are we going anywhere? You bet!

We either believe or we deny. Denial is fatal; belief is its own reward. The ups and downs, the joys and sorrows, the thrills and horrors, the trials and tests, the hills and the bumps—all are a part of the journey, and each one comes for a reason. For the man or woman who accepts this fact and confronts life's variety of good and bad exigencies, there is promised conquest. Never forget that the sun does not shine all the time. Sometimes there is rain, sometimes storms with wind and hail and floods, but through it all He is working His plan. As long as we understand this we can face anything with patience and confidence. Nothing is happenstance. You and I are in the design of the Lord for the redemption of all creation.

Following are some Scripture passages confirming the thesis of this book. Read them not once, but often, that the seriousness of living be not overlooked or forgotten.

> Fear God and keep His commandments; for this is the whole duty of man. For God shall bring every work into judgment, with every secret thing, whether it be good, or whether it be evil. (Ecclesiastes 12:13-14)

> He hath shown thee, O man, what is good; and what doth the Lord require of thee, but to do justly, and to love mercy, and to walk humbly with thy God? (Micah 6:8)

> For what shall it profit a man, if he shall gain the whole world, and lose his own soul? or what shall a man give in exchange for his soul? (Mark 8:36-37)

Whosoever heareth these sayings of mine, and doeth them, I will liken him unto a wise man, who built his house upon a rock. And the rain descended, and the floods came, and the winds blew and beat upon that house, and it fell not; for it was founded upon a rock. And everyone that heareth these sayings of mine, and doeth them not, shall be likened unto a foolish man, who built his house upon the sand. And the rain descended, and the floods came, and the winds blew and beat upon that house, and it fell; and great was the fall of it. (Matthew 7:24-27)

Think it not strange concerning the fiery trial which is to test you, as though some strange thing happened unto you, but rejoice, inasmuch as ye are partakers of Christ's sufferings, that, when his glory shall be revealed, ye may be glad also with exceeding joy. (1 Peter 4:12-13)

Count it all joy when ye fall into divers temptations, knowing this, that the trying of your faith worketh patience. But let patience have her perfect work, that ye may be perfect and entire, wanting nothing. (James 1:2-4)

There hath no temptation taken you but such as is common to man; but God is faithful, who will not permit you to be tempted above that ye are able, but will, with the temptation, also make the way to escape, that ye may be able to bear it. (1 Corinthians 10:13)

Blessed are ye, when men shall revile you, and persecute you, and shall say all manner of evil against you falsely, for my sake. Rejoice, and be exceedingly glad;

for great is your reward in heaven; for so persecuted they the prophets who were before you. (Matthew 5:11-12)

Work out your own salvation with fear and trembling. For it is God who worketh in you both to will and to do of his good pleasure. Do all things without murmurings and disputings, that you may be blameless and harmless, children of God, without rebuke, in the midst of a crooked and perverse nation, among whom ye shine as lights in the world. (Philippians 2:12-15)

Endure hardness, as a good soldier of Jesus Christ. No man that warreth entangleth himself with the affairs of this life, that he may please him who hath chosen him to be a soldier. (2 Timothy 2:3-4)

The grace of God that bringeth salvation hath appeared to all men, teaching us that, denying ungodliness and worldly lusts, we shall live soberly, and righteously, and godly, in this present age, looking for that blessed hope, and the glorious appearing of the great God and our Savior, Jesus Christ, who gave himself for us that he might redeem us from all iniquity, and purify unto himself a people of his own, zealous of good works. (Titus 2:11-14)

Cast not away, therefore, your confidence, which hath great recompense of reward. For ye have need of patience that, after ye have done the will of God, ye might receive the promise. (Hebrews 10:35-36)

Bodily exercise profiteth little, but godliness is profitable unto all things, having promise of the life that now is and of that which is to come. (1 Timothy 4:8)

I beseech you therefore, brethren, by the mercies of God, that ye present your bodies a living sacrifice, holy, acceptable unto God, which is your reasonable service. And be not conformed to this world, but be ye transformed by the renewing of your mind, that ye may prove what is that good, and acceptable, and perfect will of God. (Romans 12:1-2)

The word which came to Jeremiah from the Lord, saying, Arise, and go down to the potter's house, and there will I cause thee to hear my words. Then I went down to the potter's house, and behold, he wrought a work on the wheels. And the vessel that he made of clay was marred in the hand of the potter; so he made it again another vessel, as seemed good to the potter to make it. Then the word of the Lord came to me saying, O house of Israel, cannot I do with you as this potter? saith the Lord. Behold, as the clay is in the potter's hand, so are ye in mine hand, O house of Israel. (Jeremiah 18:1-6)

Though our outward man perish, yet the inward man is renewed day by day. For our light affliction; which is but for a moment, worketh for us a far more exceeding and eternal weight of glory, while we look not at the things which are seen, but at the things which are not seen; for the things which are seen are temporal, but the things which are not seen are eternal. (2 Corinthians 4:16-18)

There was given to me a thorn in the flesh, the messenger of Satan to buffet me, lest I should be exalted above measure. For this thing I besought the Lord thrice, that it might depart from me. And he said unto me, My grace is sufficient for thee; for my strength is made perfect in weakness. (2 Corinthians 12:7-9)

Be thou faithful unto death, and I will give thee a crown of life. (Revelation 2:10)

I have fought a good fight, I have finished my course, I have kept the faith; henceforth there is laid up for me a crown of righteousness, which the Lord, the righteous judge, shall give me at that day; and not to me only, but unto all them also that love his appearing. (2 Timothy 4:7-8)

Engaged in a Universal Struggle

In concluding these opening remarks, it will be wise to correct some longstanding errors in our thinking. Among our many sadly mistaken ideas, taken for granted by most of us, is the assumption that someone like the Marquis de Sade is the epitome of evil while the Pope is the epitome of good with the rest of us somewhere in the middle. It is an eye-opening revelation when we realize that we all have the tendency to believe we are not really so bad (with the exception, of course, of bragging material people) as the Marquis. On the other hand, we usually think we are considerably better than we actually are. Adolph Hitler rationalized that he was restoring the glory of Germany and was essentially, therefore, doing a good thing. Hopefully, none of us is as bad as Hitler or the Marquis, but it is not a rare thing for us to rationalize about our correctness. Even the Pope accepts the awesome title, "His Holiness," as if such a thing really could be true! The only truly holy or good person is Jesus Christ. The only totally evil one is Satan. All the rest of us alike are neither wholly bad nor wholly good. We live in that vacillating mid-world between the two. When man lives his years without the regeneration of his spirit, his journey leads him down into the nether-world where eventually he becomes like Satan, for he "shall see him as he is." And, by the same token, once we are born anew into the family of God, we travel upward where finally we shall be like Christ for we "shall see *him* as he is!" It is this interval of time, this parenthesis in eternity, which begins with physical birth and ends with physical death and is given to us by God for the purpose of getting us ready to live.

Nothing would benefit the cause of Christianity more than for us to get rid of the notion that there are different classes of Christians. During one of the earlier periods of the church, it was a generally accepted view that the martyrs were superior Christians, the celibate were second in line, and the rest were *ordinary* members of the faith. What a travesty! We are all ordinary, if we are Christian at all—popes, bishops, priests, nuns, elders, presbyters, deacons, lay people—there is no difference. God forbid that this abominable caste system continue to plague us before the eyes of the world. As ordinary Christian believers, we struggle together to prepare ourselves to live with God forever. Instead of wrangling with one another over who is the best, let us humble ourselves and treat other believers who have come to know Jesus Christ as the Son of God as we would like to be treated. That is real discipleship at its most authentic point.

One additional word, please. When the Titanic began to sink, the band on board the ship was playing "Nearer My God to Thee." Our God is a longsuffering and loving heavenly Father, but we have no reason to think that we can presume on His goodness. It is a little late to start thinking about Him when the boat is going down. Yet, this is a common practice. Preparation for that day engages the whole of one's life. If Balaam wanted to "die the death of the righteous" (Numbers 23:10), he should have started thinking about it much earlier. No one dies righteous who has wasted his God-given opportunities to get ready. Life can get loaded down with superficialities that are considered to be the supreme good, while one ignores the fundamental reason he is here. And there is no greater tragedy than to "gain the whole world and lose his own soul" (Mark 8:36). The rich young fool, introduced to us by Jesus, thought he had everything he could possibly need. He had become so successful that he was the envy of his neighbors, but at that peak of worldly prosperity he plunged into the despair of death for which he was totally unprepared.   Multitudes of our families and friends go about daily living completely oblivious to the one absolute certainty of existence—death. Everyone, without exception, is 100 percent successful at dying. Yet we sedate ourselves into believing it either will not happen to us or it is so distant that we can worry about it later. Then it suddenly happens—a heart attack, an aneurysm, a stroke, a fatal accident—and we are not ready. Now is the time to begin the journey to the Father's house. Unless this is one's priority, nothing else matters. And so, off we go now into an adventure which, if approached properly and conducted correctly, will lead to the most meaningful life on earth and the glory of life everlasting.

Chapter 2

Learning to Live

The Educational Scene Today

Man has become obsessed with the need for learning. He has a near mania for acquiring as much knowledge as possible as fast as he can in this world of rapidly expanding information. Today's learning is nearly obsolete before nightfall and tomorrow's curriculum is being revised long before it is used. Any person who keeps abreast of the strides in contemporary learning needs the physical stamina of Samson, the mental powers of Solomon, and the lightning speed of Jehu.

Children start to school in private educational establishments where they are taught how to live in a group, get along with others, share their toys, and adjust to a world where parents are not at their elbows. Twelve years of learning beyond kindergarten is far from adequate in our modern world of technology. In order to achieve a place in our kind of world, every boy and girl is encouraged to get an additional four years of college. Those who plan to enter the professional or academic arena must continue their pursuits toward the master's or doctor's level. And for those who are more enterprising there is post-doctoral work, which unfortunately can lead into a career as a professional student.

With the experimentation proposed by educators in the field, many classrooms have become laboratories of confusion. In some instances, there are too many students for the number of teachers available. With so many pupils crammed together, any consistent disciplinary procedure is practically impossible. As a result, there develops an unfortunate attitude of excessive permissiveness. In such an environment, class cutting has increased, cheating is commonplace, respect for teachers has all but disappeared, and serious study is seldom a way of life. Diplomas are granted to masses of young people who are totally unprepared for the next stage in their existence. Experienced centered philosophy with growing emphasis on self-esteem as a priority is a sure way of undermining the foundations of education.

Several million students are enrolled in colleges and universities in the United States alone. It may be said that we have a bad case of college cramps, since most institutions of higher learning are overcrowded. Some are so large as to be huge cities within themselves, educational complexes where students are known more readily by numbers than by names. In some classrooms hundreds of students may be registered. Under such conditions it has become increasingly difficult to learn. The depersonalization has contributed to a breakdown of morale and a lack of needed instructor-pupil rapport.

Modern Education Has a Grievous Lack

One of the basic weaknesses in most educational philosophy and methodology lies in an objective which is shortsighted and short circuited. The final goal is either set up this side of the point of self-actualization or shorted out long before human fulfillment is achieved. Man is made for more than is usually received in the system of education as devised by today's educators. Even when one is really dedicated to a mastery of his field and not satisfied to waste his time on the exploitation of grants or scholarships, he is still not adequately prepared for what he is destined to face. This is one of the basic reasons for the expanding number of private schools and the increasing interest in home schooling.

The one thing that is included in everyone's agenda of life is death. Without exception, there are as many deaths as births—no more, no less. Eventually, for every birth recorded there will be a death certificate issued. No one except Enoch and Elijah has escaped death, and none except those who are a part of the Bride of Christ at His second coming will be spared in the future. For the rest of us, it is inevitable that death will come. Yet, there is nothing in our present program of education that even remotely prepares us for this event. A few courses are being experimented with by some colleges today, but they are only a pebble in the ocean, and most often they miss the real point completely.

It is precisely at this point where modern education suffers its greatest lack. What have we accomplished when we so carefully lay the groundwork for the few short years allotted us on this earth but completely ignore what follows? Is it that we do not really believe that life goes on beyond death? Are we actually that sure about it, or is it rather that we prefer to *act* as though there is nothing more than these "three score years and ten"?

A promising young man was asked what he planned to do with his life. Being a responsible youth, he replied that the first thing he had to do was finish his education so as to be prepared to confront the world and assume his place in it. "And what then?" he was asked.

"I suppose that I will meet a nice girl and get married," he answered. "We will build us a house and rear our children."

"And then what?"

"I will try to improve my lot in life, be promoted in my business, and lay up something for a rainy day."

"And then what?"

"As soon as the savings account is large enough to provide for our needs without further work I plan to retire. And I want to have some time left to enjoy my latter years, some time to play as much golf as I wish."

"And what then?"

"Well," said the boy with a chuckle, "Guess I'll die like everybody else."

"And what then?"

Most of us have not prepared beyond the hour of death. Some of us refuse even to think about it. After all, we are alive and strong and death seems so far away that we can mention it with a kind of nervous chuckle. Many of us know that we are not ready for death, but the whole matter is pushed aside with a plethora of things which we prefer not to face. And by ignoring it we convince ourselves that death will go away. With this irresponsible logic some of us pursue our training for the first stage of existence as though it would last forever. Only when a loved one or a close friend suddenly dies are we jolted into a confrontation with reality. And then it is only temporary. It lasts only until we can get back into the grind where such unpleasant things are forgotten. Rousseau was right when he said, "Man does not begin to think until something prevents him from acting."

Training for Something Better

Our goals can be unworthy of us. That is often the case. Our sights are set too low to bring any sense of fulfillment. Large numbers of men and women have dedicated themselves to the sole task of making a living for themselves and their families. Many of us who are older adults and who have been over the road ourselves are grieved to see our children being sucked into this false philosophy that an abundance of things insures a good life. To work hard and provide for one's family is more than commendable if it is kept within reasonable bounds, if one's definition of a living is decent subsistence and not affluent luxury. Even then the goal is far less than that for which man was made.

Sessions of evening school in practically every field of endeavor are now available for adults who wish to improve themselves in view of more lucrative levels of employment or more prestigious positions. Thus, we set up goals to surpass our attained objectives only to be as disappointed with the reaching of the new ones as we were with the realization of old ones. And it is all because our goals are far from big enough to satisfy the spiritual capacity of human life.

None of us were put here just to make a living. If there is no more to life than these few days allotted on the earth, then making a living as an end might be justified. But there is so much more! And for this reason it may be assumed that man is here to make a life. It is an easily observable fact that many people make fabulous livings without much of a life at all. Others seem to make beautiful lives on the most meager kind of living standard. There is a vast difference. Of course, one does not guarantee the other.

Shall we spend 16 or more years of schooling learning to live 70? Or shall we spend 70 learning to live forever? That is the supreme question put to every person the moment he begins to think. In a very real sense, the person who chooses the latter course of action becomes a kind of professional student himself, a course of action that may be debilitating if it is an end in itself, but it can be more than fulfilling if it has a definite goal. Such a person is constantly training for something big, an end that is not reached in this life, but an eternal goal so great as to require the best one can give during an entire lifetime. When writing to the church in Macedonia the young scholar from Tarsus said it well, "I count not myself to have apprehended, but this one thing I do, forgetting those things which are behind, and reaching forth unto those things which are before, I press toward the mark for the prize of the high calling of God in Christ Jesus" (Philippians 3:13-14).

Our days on the earth must be understood in relationship to eternity. The Christian's after death existence is the full bloom which has been predicted in the budding earthling. Therefore, our training is focused primarily upon the coming Kingdom for which we are fitted. Unless this is the case, the whole experience of earthly life has been uselessly wasted. The older one gets the more aware he becomes of this fundamental truth. To live in vain is not so much to bemoan our failure in having come to the *end* of life with nothing good in the past. It is rather to come to the *begin-*

ning of life completely unprepared to enter it! Man is in training for something big, bigger than anything he will ever experience in this world.

Helen Chappell White, as a young mother, wrote a sketch called "Something Wonderful." It concerns a young girl who always knew that something wonderful was going to happen to her someday. It had seemed very near several times. Once, as a frightened child, she was suddenly confronted by an unseen presence. Again at 14, she stood on the cupola of her grandfather's house one summer night and the stars seemed so close, almost close enough to touch. Then she fell in love, married a wonderful man, had children. What could be more wonderful? Yet, that certain something seemed to elude her, it was still in the future.

As the years passed, her children married, grandchildren came, wonderful things just kept happening. Always she seemed to sense that the best was still around the corner. Then one morning she got into her car to run to the store. A big truck came out of nowhere and crashed into her automobile. There was no time to stop, no time to swerve, no time to think. The only thing she saw was the blinding flash of reality, the certainty that at last it had happened—something wonderful!

The Value of Christian Discipline

It is one thing to be a student, to go to classes on a schedule and to engage in systematic research in a given field. It is quite another thing to be a disciple. To be sure, a disciple is a student. A student, on the other hand, may not be a disciple at all. Disciples spend enough time with a special teacher to absorb something of his or her life, something of the master's very soul as well as his or her lifestyle, and this is the one missing ingredient in the de-personalized classroom setting that characterizes most of our mammoth universities.

Jesus "chose twelve to be with him" (Mark 3:14), because the men who were to continue His mission of redemption in the world would have to be literally saturated in the Master's spirit. An academic setting where formal teaching patterns were followed would never get the job done. The Twelve would learn by association, by being with their Lord. They would live together, eat the same food, sleep on the same hard ground, and quite literally share the life and ultimate goals of Jesus. It would become second nature for the disciple who had spent three years with his teacher to develop the same outlook on life as well as to absorb the factual information contained in his lessons.

A disciple is a learner, and he learns by the discipline of doing. It is significant to note that both *disciple* and *discipline* come from the same root. One cannot become a disciple without rigorous discipline. And there was a great deal of that administered by the Lord as He patiently led the way. More than once were the Twelve corrected when their spirits were not in keeping with that of the Kingdom of Heaven. At times the correction took the form of strong rebuke.

Following the ascension of Christ, it became necessary that the Holy Spirit should be sent to "guide us into all truth" (John 16:13). Discipleship involves all of life, not just the three years which the earthly Lord was allowed with the Twelve. They were not to be left alone after the crucifixion. Soon the Holy Spirit would come on the day of Pentecost to continue the training Jesus had begun.

Every contemporary disciple of Christ has the same intimate association with Jesus as that enjoyed by the chosen ones of long ago, for the Holy Spirit testifies of Christ and disciplines us. Those objectives which were Christ's are held before us so we might bring ourselves into line with the final goal of God. The Twelve were so sure of the ultimate end for which man is made that they were unafraid to have their earthly lives cut short by martyrdom. The Lord had gone "to prepare a place" (John 14:1) for them, and nothing temporal could interfere with that eternal destination. They were convinced that they had been born for that hour and that every earth bound experience should be seen in that perspective.

Several years ago it was my good fortune to be permitted to tour some of the countries of Europe. Being curious, but not very courageous, it took some time before I admitted my ignorance and asked an English guide the meaning of the little window stickers with the letter L attached to nearly every automobile on the streets of London. It was explained that the drivers of those cars did not have their permanent driver's licenses as yet, that they had been issued a learner's permit. The very fact that there were so many with these probationary permits only served to illustrate a much greater truth. We are all learners in the school of life. We are learners as long as we live. No one ever reaches the place where the Lord does not seek to discipline and develop him in his journey toward the far distant goal.

What Are We Learning?
Paul warns young Timothy about those who are "ever learning and never able to come to a knowledge of the truth" (2 Timothy 3:7). What a parody on learning it is when we

amass great quantities of information about a thousand and one things without ever discovering what life is all about.

Some of us have learned how to turn into gold almost everything we touch. We have mastered the available sources of knowledge in our field of labor and we are smug in our accomplishments. We have found out how to manipulate people themselves for our own selfish ends. We have the world on a string and the string around our finger. Nothing but blue skies. Everything is going our way. Life could not get any better. There is every reason to be supremely happy. But that is just the problem.

While we have learned all these arts we seem to have lost our souls. Our marriages are breaking apart, our children despise us, the family unit is coming unglued, and even our friends suspect our motives. Inside, there is an utter emptiness that none of our learning seems to touch. The sense of purpose so essential to going on with life has taken wings, and we are left floundering in the mire of meaninglessness. By now we should know how to get the very best out of life, but nothing we do brings lasting satisfaction. For some of us, it gets so bad that 50,000 people commit suicide every year rather than face what they have become. Our culture is the most affluent, the most knowledgeable, the most cosmopolitan, the most sophisticated ever in recorded history, but we are also the most wretched and the most miserably confused.

Our learning is of no ultimate value or personal satisfaction if it is not anchored to Him who is the Truth. Until our objectives, motivations, and methods for living are grounded in the eternal absolute—the living Christ—we have joined those who are "ever learning but never able to come to a knowledge of the truth." Unless there is a concentrated focus on the end for which we were born, it would have been better never to have been born at all. The goal is not worth the effort unless the goal is eternal life.

If we could ask the men, who lived with Jesus for three years and then shared His continuing presence in the Holy Spirit for the rest of their days, what they learned, their answer might be surprising for our materialistic age. Their values were so different that they appear to have had no interest in the possessions, positions, and prestige that had once overpowered them. What they had found in their discipleship had so totally transformed their perspective that they could hardly believe the world was the same. But it was not the world that had been altered—it was their own souls, their own minds, their own way of looking at life and discovering its purpose.

Those early disciples were learning to *be*. The basic stuff for them was not to be pampered, prosperous, or prominent. It was just to be, to be what God created them to be, to be like Jesus and finally to share the promise of the Father, which is to live forever. Shakespeare was absolutely right: "To be or not to be, that is the question." To be a part of the family of God, an eternal Kingdom of righteousness, a community of love and truth which endures forever— that is what it means to be. Anything else is a tragedy—it is not to be

Before meeting Jesus there was not a single man among the Twelve who recognized who he was apart from the *things* he possessed. By these things he identified himself. Once the Lord had opened their eyes and ears to the loving nature of God and the rebel nature of man, their grip on their self-sufficiency began to relax and they breathed more easily. What a relief it was to know that man was not bound and gagged by a maze of traditions and laws that promised nothing but judgment. If God loved them and cared about their problems, then they could and would love Him. What a difference it made!

No longer were they defensive. It was not necessary to argue for their position. They really had no position to do battle for, just a marvelous story of joy and peace to tell. Matthew had found something better than his money. Simon had discovered a welcome release from his hatred of Rome. Nathanael found the Truth he had been struggling for all his life. They had all learned to trust, to believe, and to love. Saul himself discovered how wonderful it was to be able to breathe the fresh air of freedom, freedom from the thraldom of law, freedom in the service of a Master who in love had redeemed him from the clutches of slavery. None of these men had known how to live until they met Jesus. Like masses around the world today, they were living for the wrong things. And all because nobody had ever shown them how to be different. No one else could.

Now the disciples had learned that "eye hath not seen, nor ear heard, neither have entered into the heart of man, the things which God hath prepared for them that love him" (1 Corinthians 2:9). No more did they worry about the future since Jesus had assured them, "In my Father's house are many mansions: If it were not so, I would have told you. I go to prepare a place for you. And if I go to prepare a place for you, I will come again and receive you unto myself; that where I am, there ye may be also" (John 14:1-3). And no matter what happened to the world and those things of earth to which they had so tenaciously clung, they now looked forward to the "new heaven and the new earth"

(Revelation 21:1) "wherein dwelleth righteousness" (2 Peter 3:13).

Life's Periodic Quizzes

Almost imperceptibly, life has a way of checking on what we have learned. None of us are permitted to live our allotted years without at least one or two checkups. Sometimes one does not recognize these exigencies as tests at all, but they are precisely that. We may or may not be warned that our level of learning is about to be examined.

In the disastrous national depression of the early 1930s many persons faced a severe episode of personal adversity. It was a testing of the greatest magnitude. Multitudes of people panicked when they discovered their stocks, bonds, and bank accounts worthless. Obviously, in spite of their earlier successes, they had really learned nothing at all about life. Jesus had clearly said, "A man's life consisteth not in the abundance of things which he possesses" (Luke 12:15). Man ought to know that by now. But we are incurably slow to learn fundamental lessons that life seeks to teach us.

The Christian ought not to find it such a shattering experience when he fails to get the promotion which was anticipated. Even a demotion will not dismember him emotionally. As these words are written, a young man, who had expected to be promoted in his job but was disappointed, has killed himself. There were probably other circumstances involved that precipitated such a drastic remedy to the problem, but failure in business was undoubtedly a part of it. Financial hardship, though uncomfortable to bear, has many valuable lessons to teach. In it all, we learn that one can trust the Lord even when he does not know what the future holds. May it not be that

God allows such hardship to check on us, to see whether we have learned to depend on Him when we cannot handle our own problems? None of us can begin to fathom the mystery underlying the untimely death of a child, or the breakup of a love relationship, or the crash of a financial nest egg, or any one of a thousand unwanted interruptions that seek to undo us. The crucial thing, however, is not whether we understand what happens, but how we react to it. Do we learn anything from it? Or do we just grow bitter and negative about God and life in general? Anyone can blow his cork and accuse God of being unfair or declare life to be a meaningless blur. Not until one has come to know God as Jesus revealed Him and to accept life as a proving ground where our metal is tested, is there the possibility that we will learn anything in our adversities.

An opportunity for deciding between the two alternatives discussed in the preceding paragraph is the prospect of one's own death or the diagnosis of a terminal illness. As these words are being written the body of an elderly saint of God has just been laid to rest in Alabama. When we first met Grace she was a bubbly widow whose radiance spilled over on everyone she touched. For as long as her friends could remember, she had taught the Bible class in her local church. Just being with this dear child of God was a benediction in itself. Everyone loved Grace, and Grace loved everyone. There was nothing she enjoyed more than talking about the Bible, unless it was talking about her Lord. No one ever wondered where she would go when she died, because she was already there. A few months before she died, Grace called us one evening to tell us what she had just found out. The doctor had diagnosed her with terminal leukemia. The usual sound to follow the report of such a disclosure would have been sobbing on the other end of the line. But, was Grace sobbing? Not on your life! She was exuberant. "I've got leukemia! Isn't that wonderful! I am soon going to be with my Lord!" Those were the joyful words that thrilled us through and through as we heard this radiant spirit confront the news of her coming death.

To confront such uncertainties in strong confidence that suffering can be redemptive, and thus a part of the good design of God, is proof that one has received a passing grade on the quiz. For some, like Grace, it is not just a passing grade— it is graduation with highest honors. On the other hand, we have all seen professing Christians go to pieces when presented with the prospects of surgery or prolonged illness. To react in such manner is to show up poorly on the periodic examination.

Losing a loved one in death is probably the most traumatic experience any of us will ever have to face. It is natural to weep and to grieve at the initial shock of the death of someone whom we have loved. But to display a lack of confidence in God by continuous somberness and dejection is far from the normal response for a Christian believer. If our lessons have been learned well, we will be prepared well enough not to be caught off guard. Even death is a part of the divine design and, at such times, one's relationship to and confidence in a sovereign God is either strengthened or denied. These occasional life situation quizzes are far from easy, but they must be taken. And only they who keep up with their daily discipleship are able to take them in stride.

Learning to Be Free

To the Jewish believers Jesus said, "If you continue in my word, you are truly my disciples, and you will know the truth, and the truth will make you free" (John 8:31-32). To be delivered from sin and the bondage of the law, is to be wholly free to be the kind of self the Creator intended. It is to be fully human, to have the image and likeness of God (which has been effaced by sin) restored. Regardless as to what else one may have learned, until he has discovered the essential meaning of salvation from the curse of sin, he has not looked straight into the face of truth itself.

Jesus Christ is incarnate truth, that is, divine truth in human flesh. For this reason He could emphatically declare, "I am the way, the truth, and the life" (John 14:6). For anyone else to have said that, would have been blasphemy. Today there are multiplied millions of people who are certain beyond any doubt that Jesus Christ was and is exactly what He said. In the school of life a man must learn more than information relating to what the great philosophers have said about life. He must come to know life itself. This is why the Lord explained the earlier statement about freedom in truth with an additional and more personal one, "If the Son makes you free, you shall be free indeed" (John 8:36). Christ is truth. In knowing Him, somehow we naturally come to recognize the truth about all of life, which sets us free to love, believe, and serve.

One of the most illuminating words ever spoken about the relatedness of real living to real truth has been recorded by Matthew. Jesus was speaking to the multitudes: "Come unto me, all you who labor and are heavy laden, and I will give you rest. Take my yoke upon you, and learn of me; for I am meek and lowly in heart, and you will find rest for your souls. For my yoke is easy, and my burden is light" (Matthew 11:28-30). It is quite interesting, and most unfortunate, that masses of men and women continue to lug around their burdens and try to pull the whole load when sharing everything with Christ would lighten the weight and illumine the spirit. In a shared discipleship, which puts us in the same harness, we learn what life is all about. And we discover how to enjoy it without the fears and pressures which accompany some who think everything depends hopelessly on their own human strength and wisdom.

Learning to live is a lifetime pursuit that begins the moment we find Christ and culminates at the moment of physical death. And he who has "so learned Christ" (Ephesians 4:20) here will be truly ready to live beyond the grave where the dimensions of existence will be magnified without limit. What we have been sharing in this chapter is beyond the realm of speculation. This is not a philosophical subject. There is nothing abstract about learning to live. We are on solid ground here. No one should be less than concrete when discussing life and how it is acquired and developed. As Christians, we have the answer to the big question. We know why we are here. And we know what to do about it.

— Chapter 3 —

Why Are We Here?

A Human Analysis of The Divine Motive

Often we hear someone ask why God made man. At times the scope of the question has been broadened to include a reason for the universe as well. It goes without saying that no one can presume to know the mind of the divine Creator, nor can any claim either the right or the power to psycho-analyze God! We do well to hear the admonishment of ancient Job by the Creator: "Who is this that darkeneth counsel by words without knowledge?" (Job 38:2). But if such curiosity does not become an obsession that excludes simple saving faith, there is no sin in discussing the baffling matter. Frankly, it is not likely that any sane adult could live out his days without entertaining such a thought at least once.

It is inconceivable that the Lord who made heaven and earth would have done so without reason. Non-theistic science would insist that there is no reason for either man or his universe. And if there is no creating God, such would be inevitably correct. But once God enters the picture everything changes. Nothing is left to chance. The world and the human race become reasonable. Our problem in deciphering that reason lies in the limitation of human knowledge. However, while He, whose ways are past finding out and whose judgments are unsearchable (Romans 11:33), is not obligated to reveal more than He wills, is it possible that some hint may have been left for us? Could the Scriptures contain any clues?

According to recorded biblical history, the first thing God did was to create the earth with its seas, its heavens, its vegetation, and its conscious animal life. No one can say what the Creator may have done before that moment. Our times begin with that divine act, and there is no suggestion as to whether He who made us engaged in any act of creation other than that of the angels prior to the making of our world. To seek information beyond that point is to descend into hollow speculation.

The supreme act of God was that of making a creature like unto Himself, that is, man in His divine image. Although there were many other creatures of flesh upon the earth, the Creator observed that man was quite alone. He was one of a kind. Nothing already made in the animal kingdom was suitable for man's companion. Such a companion would have to be enough like Adam to be recognizable as the other half of the whole —man's alter ego. The solution was Eve and, although man's frustrations were just beginning, his loneliness was over.

The question that naturally arises is how the Creator knew that "it is not good that the man should be alone" (Genesis 2:18). Of course, if He is God He knows everything. But that is an oversimplification of the question. Conceivably, man himself may have been created because

God was lonely. At once, someone will interrupt us to say that human attributes must not be levied on the Eternal Spirit. However, if God is a personal Being, there is no way for us to begin thinking of Him or declaring Him to others than by the use of human traits, limited as they may be. Therefore, we do our heavenly Father no injustice to ascribe to Him the emotion of loneliness.

Neither the celestial hosts nor the angelic beings afforded the companionship desired by the Creator. And since it is the nature of God to share Himself and His love, He created man in His likeness to communicate and enter into creative partnership with him. If this surmise is true, then the Eternal Spirit made man for the same reason He created Eve. In the first instance, it was to avoid *divine* loneliness. In the second, it was to avoid *human* loneliness.

We may assume that man was the end the Lord had in mind when the universe itself was made. If so, the earth was created in order that God would have a place to put His new partner. And this brings us to the very important aspect of the God-man relationship. There is a kind of two-pronged purpose in the whole thing since, while the earth was made for man, man was created for the earth. Moses informs us that "the Lord God took the man and put him in the garden of Eden to dress it and to keep it" (Genesis 2:15). Adam was to "have dominion over the fish of the sea, and over the fowl of the air, and over every living thing that moves upon the earth" (Genesis 1:28) as well as authority over the earth itself.

When earthly parents bring a child into the world they share the motivation that moved the Creator. The child is the product of love (unless the role of sex is permitted to be prostituted) and is brought into existence in order that the mother and father may cherish and love him. It is also the desire of the parents that their offspring, made in their own likeness, will carry on the life and work they have begun. Thus, we see that the continuous creation of human life is the result of a desire not to be alone, a compulsion to love, and a hope of perpetuity. Nothing pleases a mother and father more than to see their offspring fulfilling their dream for loving communion within the family. An added benefit is the assurance that children will be a credit to the family name. Reflected in human reproduction is a faint but unmistakable duplication of the divine motive.

Where Do We Go from Here?

If we admit that the above attempt at a solution to the enigma of man's creation is about as good as we can come up with, what can be said beyond this point of initial creativity? Is human life only the plaything of deity? Are we just mechanical robots manipulated for the pleasure of a God who has nothing better to do with His time? Are we puppets on a string, whose delightful movements and miserable actions alike are destined by some distant puppeteer who is greatly entertained by it all? Why are we here? Or better yet, why are we *still* here? After all, in light of the havoc and unpleasantness that seem to attend our existence, it is remarkable that we are yet around.

Has the Creator just made us and turned us loose to find our way as best we can, or does He still care about what is happening in His world? If He does care, then why does He not do something about war, poverty, and injustice? Why is human life such a sordid thing if it is possible for it to be different? Is this brief heartache all there is or is there something more than most of us realize to this business of living? These are typical of the maze of questions man asks himself today.

The emptiness and boredom, not to mention the outright rebellion, felt by multitudes of people in our day is glaring proof that we have lost our way. Like lost sheep that have wandered aimlessly away from the sheepfold and cannot find their way back, the human race has strayed far from God. Being out of touch with the divine Shepherd, it is impossible to have either a sense of security or an awareness of destiny. When man is away from his Creator, he is lonely as was God prior to the creation of man.

This being the case, human goals are established which are far less than man can achieve in his own strength and wisdom. Frustration evolves from a built-in awareness of having substituted our objectives for those of the Creator and also from our inability to reach even the substitutes. Continual chaos breeds such discontent that millions of people ask why they are here.

Man-Made Utopias

Like the ancient descendants of Noah, who tried to build a heaven on earth without regard to God, contemporary man is bent on erecting his own structured utopia (Genesis 11). When once man has become estranged from his Creator, he is forced either to be self-sufficient or to return in repentance to the God whom he has wronged. The general pattern in our time is to succumb to human pride and prove that we can provide our own heaven, that man does not need to rely on any supernatural power. What is being called heaven is a strange thing to behold. The Great Society turned out to be a total failure. And the New World Order is destined for the same scrap heap.

The original plan to form a federation of countries loosely bound together in our present world organization is an oft-repeated step in the direction of one world government. Of course, it will never work. Ingrained in the fabric of the world's governments is the thread of evil which thwarts man's highest dream for universal brotherhood. As long as that thread remains a part of the tapestry of earthly kingdoms, there can be no finally acceptable world rule. State leaders may succeed in temporarily postponing war on a grand scale, but the day of universal judgment will finally come.

The biblical account of the tower of Babel (Genesis 11) indicates that God is displeased with any man-made plan which would unify all peoples in a world government of sin. He does not will that man should be united in the perpetuation of evil. The creation of nations was the divine means of negating such a disastrous course of action. And while national leaders are determined to build a utopia of world power and peace, the seed of monstrous decay which that utopia would bring lie ready to sprout. Only the wise intervention of God prohibits its happening.

Related to the world government idea is the plot to create a monolithic religious structure. The subtle thrust of the ecumenical movement is directed toward a united church. No one could possibly object to the spirit of ecumenicity which has made us all more tolerant of each other's religious differences. But to set up a needless union of ecclesiastical bodies based on an almost purely humanistic objective is neither Christian nor sensible. In the years since the origin of the council, whose aim is to bring all religions into one conglomerate union, the philosophy of the world church has grown less and less biblical. The cooperative and appreciative spirit which exists among varied church groups in a typical community setting seems to have developed independently of the influence of such a council and to lack any affinity with it.

In the foreseeable future, we may witness the ushering in of the rule of Antichrist, the end-time political ruler of the world. Not without grounds is the suggestion that the appearance of this dreaded empire of Antichrist will be aided by the two world organizations mentioned above. In fact, the beast himself may well arise out of the world government organization, while the false prophet, who will assist him, evolves into some kind of supreme head of the union of ecclesiastical bodies. Should this be so, then we already have the groundwork laid for the debut of "the man of sin" (2 Thessalonians 2:3). Man's human utopias are only deceptive mirages in the wasteland of evil. There will never be social, political, or religious perfection as long as humanity remains imperfect. To expect any such conditions is to live in an imaginary world where we refuse to face reality. None of this is to suggest that Christians should not affirm their hope for and dedicate their efforts toward a better world, but it is to say that all our struggles combined can never usher in the Kingdom of God.

Existing For Today

There is a wild race all around us today for social and financial preeminence. Everybody wants a bigger house than he has. Many of us want high-powered cars, the most expensive electronic gadgets, and a big chunk of the stock market. But that is only the beginning of what we want. We have learned to want such things because our affluent society has taught us that one's importance is guaged by his superiority in material possessions, by the cubic inch displacement under the hood of his car, by the upper class stores where he purchases the best brand names on the market.

It is true that some young people have gone to the other extreme. Having seen the miserable shell in which their affluent parents live, they dress in shabby clothes and live a disheveled lifestyle. Often such youths have only exchanged the status symbol from material to physical things. Their importance is not measured by stocks and property but by drugs and sex.

Everything is geared to the *now*. Ours is called the Now Generation. Even the Christian faith has been all but emasculated of its eternal hope by an emphasis on the here and now. Clergymen hardly ever refer to heaven or hell, to man's immortal spirit, or to the joys or miseries of life after death. Anyone who does insist on the importance of the next world must expect to be laughed at because the only way to discover what life is all about is by forgetting the future and concentrating on the now. As man knows, in his saner moments, this philosophy is right enough to be attractive and wrong enough to be deadly.

Technology is responsible for automation which has relieved man of tremendous amounts of hard labor and reduced his working hours. His wages have increased and he has more of the things coveted by human beings everywhere. His house is larger, his garage now houses two cars and a golf cart, and his vacations are more luxurious than ever. With spiraling increases in the cost of everything, however, he always feels the all pervading pressure of not keeping pace with the increasing desires of his family. Bankruptcy is only a day away and everything he has is mortgaged to the hilt. Taxes are becoming an intolerable burden and, if the trend continues, he knows that he will someday be paying as much in taxes as he earns in wages. With all his improved conditions, man is unable to plan sensibly for tomorrow and he is miserable trying to live today. Obviously, there are exceptions to this generality, but such commentary is tragically accurate when looking at modern people as a whole.

Since the future is so uncertain, the average man in today's world has succumbed to the stifling philosophy of hedonism. Why not live for today if there is no tomorrow? He only goes around once, and then it is all over. Unless he grabs what he can now, it may pass him forever. So he falls into a life of pleasure seeking as if pleasure were going out of style.

Were we to ask this man why he is here, he would argue that the chief end of life is that one enjoy himself. This life of self-gratification is the exact opposite of what men of an earlier day believed to be the reason for human existence. For them man was here "to glorify God and enjoy Him forever." To enjoy God is not the same thing as enjoying oneself. No one wishes to endorse the plaintive Puritanism, which condemned anything that was pleasurable. But the all too common emphasis, even within the church, that self-gratification under the guise of divinely appointed self- esteem is the objective of Christianity is more than suspect. If God is the chief end of man's life, every day will be monitored by an awareness of divine surveillance. If man is his own end, then there is no possible reason why he should not "eat, drink, and be merry," especially in view of his certain death.

Short-Range Goals for a Misspent Life

One of the immediate objectives for masses of people both young and old is that of sexual gluttony. Sociologists are now warning us that marriage is on the way out. Extramarital affairs are commonplace and premarital sex is becoming a way of life. Spouse swapping has grown into a widespread middle class American custom. Many business and professional men have harems, although they do not live together in the same building. Housewives find it convenient to get involved with other men. College students have free access to both men's and women's dormitories, and growing numbers of them live together until the new wears off. Then they settle down with other exciting possibilities. High schools are filled with sexually experienced young people who see no future in growing up and getting married because they have already tried everything. Even junior high boys and girls often know more about the intimacies of sexual love than their parents. Virginity and chastity are laughed at and joked about as if those who practice such a lifestyle are living in the wrong period of history, as if they were an anachronism. Ours has become a culture of free love with little or no responsibility.

The mass media continues to flood our minds with the prestige of sex. Radio and television commercials are enhanced by sex. Books and magazines are piled high on almost every bookseller's rack in which the idea is enforced that you are a nobody unless you have sex as often as you eat and with as many people as you meet. A young teenage girl who came seeking counsel admitted to having engaged in sexual intercourse with a boy whom she did not even particularly like. Her reason was that she was ashamed to be a virgin! With the constant brainwashing confronted by young people today, it is possible for one to confuse what is virtue and what is not. For that matter, the view endorsed by our morally depraved culture is that it does not matter anyway.

There is a shocking openness about this obsession with sex. No one seems to feel any embarrassment about it at all. Erotic and obscene films are shown in theaters all across the nation, movies that were formerly seen only in bawdy houses. Four-letter words now appear in sophisticated literature, words that were formerly inscribed on public toilet walls. Pornography is looked upon as a viable option for respectable people who want to live in open smut. Gay people blatantly boast of their perversion as a valid form of sexuality. Women have become as coarse as the most debased men used to be. Contraceptives and condoms are available for anyone, and there is no embarrassment in asking for them. Abstinence is no longer the norm for the unmarried. The norm is *safe* sex. Young people retain a mental back door clause in their marriage ceremony (if there is any marriage at all) so that they will not feel guilty if sex does not meet their expectations and they are forced to get a divorce. Divorces and annulments constitute a big part of the baggage that weighs so heavily on a declining culture.

In addition to sex, there is still an enormous alcohol problem, which, while giving a sense of release from life's hard places, cripples hundreds of thousands of men and women in their abilities to face life realistically. Yet, liquor flows freely across the land and many people feel that they are not an acceptable part of their peer groups unless they drink enough to overcome all inhibitions that would hamper their being fully animal. We are fast becoming a nation of drunkards.

As if the liquor scourge were not enough, we now have millions of people experimenting with drugs. The sense of euphoria, the levitation of the soul, and the trips into a world of fantasy seem to be the only goal left for some of the world's most tragic individuals. Life consists for these people in having a fling in the face of all the medical warnings of the land. Young lives are thrown away in a moment of weakness and multitudes of our sons and daughters never find their way out of the unreal world of addiction. Their minds and bodies succumb to an abnormal existence which leads into deep depression and living death. Yet, this kind of goal appears to be the only thing for which some people live.

The story of drugs does not stop with our youth. Parents and older adults, particularly those in upper-income brackets, spend a fortune on stimulants or tranquilizers prescribed by physicians who can find no organic problem. The pressure and tension from fast living, affluence, and social competition have made such wrecks of us that we must numb ourselves to get through the day and sedate ourselves to sleep at night. Our goals are too small for us and achieved too quickly. Beyond these unworthy goals, multitudes see nothing worth living for at all.

No Exit

Being imprisoned in this kind of now-or-never world, millions of men and women are convinced that there is really no way out. The human race is hemmed in on every side and there is no escape into some heaven up above or some hell down below. For masses of people anything would be better than where they are now. Man is shoved into this world by some accident which he does not even remember and he leaves it in the same manner. He is a victim of a thousand conditions that determine everything he does and says. Being born under a particular star sign is believed to shape irrevocably the entire earthly life of an individual. Everything is cut and dried and predetermined, and there is nothing anyone can do to alter that fate.

If there were just some ray of hope, some hint that the direction which our lives take has some significance. Masses of people complain that they cannot find an answer to their questions about the meaning of life. All they hear is the echo of their own voices. A prevalent philosophy espoused by multitudes (who do not know that the high sounding word describes their style of life) is existentialism. For the existentialist, life has no eternal significance whatsoever. We are all victims caught in the web of complex circumstances and there is no reason to expect anything better. Though he may outwardly appear happy enough, the real existentialist is as pessimistic about ever discovering any meaning to living as was Schopenaur. This philosopher believed that life is one continuous bout with boredom and frustration and that all pleasure is only temporary respites from the inevitable monotony of human survival.

Death is a relief to people like those we have been describing, not because they envision something better in the world to come, but because it puts an end to meaninglessness. There being no purpose in either living or dying, the latter is the more coveted state since it renders one wholly unconscious of the hollowness in which he is otherwise destined to suffer. Since nothing awaits man in the world to come, nothing that happens here can make any essential difference. And death itself is only the other end of an animate period which began with birth, neither the beginning nor the ending having any meaning.

Much of what is written for today's theater is deliberately absurd. That is why we may watch a play or see a movie and feel completely undone at the end. The plot seems so vague as to be moving toward no predesigned end. Nothing really seems to happen and, when it is over, nothing has made any sense at all. The mood of frustration is what the playwright has intended to create in the audience. It is his belief that life is this way and that any other kind of portrayal would be dishonest and unrealistic. This kind of artistic expression is what we call the theater of the absurd.

Much of what passes for advanced art is unintelligible, disordered, and ugly to most people. There are always the intellectually elite who will make every effort to explain some of the surreal stuff which has been splashed on a canvas. A classic story is told about a man staring intently at an art display with a puzzled look on his face. Seeing the uninitiated spectator with the glazed expression in his eyes, a self-proclaimed expert quickly came to his rescue. Removing his pipe from his mouth and tilting his head knowingly to one side, the expert condescendingly explained all the lines, shades, and nuances of the grotesque painting. Just as the interpreter was reaching his most graphic level of excitement, the museum curator appeared, excused himself, and turned the painting right side up!

It is not because the uninitiated are too low-brow to appreciate the finer things of life that much artistic expression fails to move them. Rather it is due to the fact that artists who are responsible for these abstract and cubist creations are aware that there is something wrong with life in our world. Life for them is out of focus and the harmony of divine creation is absent from the cacophony of the modern scene. Life for many people is all mixed up, an assortment of meaningless events and experiences. The song in *The Mikado* is definitive of much contemporary living as "a thing of shreds and patches". Don Marquis was on the same wavelength when he suggested that life is "like a scrambled egg."

The older generation has more than a little difficulty in understanding the music being sung by our youth. This is nothing new. Such has always been the case with what is known as the generation gap. Today's gap, however, seems to be more pronounced. Not alone is it hard to understand the words themselves, but the bulk of it is loud, mournful, and sad. One has an indescribable feeling of emptiness and disenchantment after having listened to it. But this is also a commentary on a people who have lost their way and can find no continuous thread of meaning which ties their years together and gives purpose for continuing to exist.

Getting the Most out of Life

Christianity has insisted from the beginning that life has a definite meaning. The Creator has put us on the earth for a purpose. Every man's birth holds great potential and his death should open wider doors to being. There is a divine plan for each individual. God has before His eyes a schema or blueprint for every person who has ever lived. Not everyone finds or develops that print into a reality. But when that plan is discovered and fulfilled, every experience becomes a joyous milestone of purposeful progress. The human race is going somewhere and each person can move toward a glorious consummation. Jesus had this in mind when He warned against forgetting that we are citizens of two worlds: "What shall it profit a man if he gain the whole world and lose his own soul?" (Mark 8:36).

Earth's short day is seen in a different light when it is understood as an initial stage in an eternal design. The Christian faith builds on the presupposition, as affirmed by Christ Himself, that these threescore years and ten comprise only the first chapter in the story of life that has no end. An even better analogy would be to compare human existence to the prelude, not even the first chapter, of a grand plot requiring all eternity to complete. Man on the earth is just getting ready to live. He is preparing for the epic of the ages, the divine design toward which all creation has moved since the beginning of the world. The paradise lost in Eden will be restored in heaven and man, whose misery stems from being separate from his Creator, can again be a part of the family of God as he was meant to be before the fall into sin.

It is possible to get everything out of life or it is possible to get nothing. The difference lies in one's response to the plan or God. Either we leave God out of the world and live our lives in a vacuum of utter meaninglessness, or we admit the sovereignty of the Lord and work in union with His gradually but perfectly developing plan for the redemption of creation. The latter course is one which rests on faith in the truth about life, as revealed by Jesus Christ, and it is the only approach to existence that makes sense. Every man must make his own choice and accept the consequences in both this world and the next.

When Tolstoy was about 50, he discovered life becoming increasingly dull and void of purpose. For two years he was haunted by what Ecclesiastes calls the *vanity* of living.

Tempted with thoughts of self extinction, he would not allow a gun near him for fear that he might shoot himself. He even hid other instruments of hurt that they might not, by their ready availability, seduce him into physical annihilation. Then, as he was walking in the woods, he found new thoughts of God milling about in his brain, thoughts which he could not account for at all. When he thought of God, however, he noted that his heart grew still and his mind found release from his depression. Then it dawned on him that God is all about us, and that the reason life becomes meaningful when God is recognized is because God is life itself. Therefore, in the inner sanctuary of his own soul he sought God and His accompanying blessing of peaceful purpose. Sounds much like Augustine who was sure that the Creator had made man for Himself and that no man could ever find rest unless that rest were found in God.

An illustration of this fundamental truth can be gleaned from the Old Testament in the call and pilgrimage of Abraham. After his call in Ur of the Chaldees, Abraham was never the same again. God had made a great promise, a divine covenant, that through this faithful disciple a kingdom with eternal dimensions would be born. There were times when the patriarch's faith was not as strong as it ought to have been, but he never lost sight of the end for which the call had come. Thus every incident, whether good or bad, was viewed as a stepping stone which would ultimately lead to the fulfillment of the promise. Life had meaning for Abraham because there was a definite purpose for his pilgrimage. He would have rejected Christopher Morley's definition of life as "a game of whist between Man and Nature." There was no chance involved in Abraham's life, no such thing as luck. It was not a game the outcome of which was unknown, but it was a well planned partnership between a sovereign and loving God and an obedient and faithful man. Indeed, that is what life is all about. That is why we are here.

Chapter 4

The Trial Run

Conversion As a Process

When a small boy was asked who made him, he replied, "I ain't done yet!" And he was right. No man is a finished product. As long as we live we are in the process of being made. Creation always has a beginning, a moment when that which is to be is actually started. When God began to create the heavens and the earth, it was with the intent that nothing would be static but that everything would exist in a continuing state of creation. The earth is new every morning, daily renewing itself. Though the Lord rested on the seventh day, this should not be construed to mean that He terminated and finalized it all. He did not henceforth stand back and leave the world alone like a watchmaker waiting for the watch to run down. It is only as He acts upon what has been made that it remains alive and fresh. Creation is a progressive thing. The fiat to be was given by God on the morning of creation, but the order to become was written into the earth, the sea, and the sky. In no way is this truth to be mistaken for the erroneous theory of evolution, which is unbiblical and scientifically untenable. Evolution and creation are mutually exclusive. I am simply, but categorically, insisting that creation is dynamic, vigorous, forceful, and intense.

What is true of the earth is likewise true of man himself. Man's body is completely replaced every seven years. Thus he is a new man at recurring intervals in his earthly pilgrimage. It is God who preserves and sustains us, not like some inanimate mass that retains its shape and size, but as living creatures in whom has been infused the image of the Creator. And if this is true of the rejuvenation of the flesh of man throughout his lifetime, it is to be assumed that the situation would be much the same as relates to man's spirit.

Conversion, like creation, is progressive. It is more than coincidental that Paul, when writing about conversion, exclaims, "If any man be in Christ he is a new *creation*" (2 Corinthians 5:17). In reality, the term *conversion* is descriptive of the commencement of spiritual life even as the word *creation* is descriptive of the beginning of physical existence. Yet, in both instances, that which has its point of genesis is also continuous. Every man "must be born again" (John 3:7) but that is just a place to start. That which happens at the moment of the new birth is the beginning of a progressive state of being converted until the time of death. And there is no reason to assume that the Christian will stop growing and developing even then, though the time of conversion will be over. God has His hands on us and He continues throughout the years to bring us through one new conversion of our ways and attitudes after another. It was Leighton who said it for us, "The stones which God means to make resplendent He often has His tools upon."

There is only one new birth, but there are many conversions for the person who walks with God.

The little boy answered well the question about having been made. Had he said that God made him he would have been correct. But his awareness that he was still being made adds considerable weight to our understanding of the nature of creation.

Getting the Bugs Out

Often we hear someone say of some new product which he has purchased, "It's difficult to buy anything anymore that does not have bugs in it." Admittedly, such a person might be talking about the unhappy experience of having found worms in the corn meal. Such a discovery is rare, however, and the complaint probably has to do with some manufactured article with mechanical moving parts. It may be an automobile, an appliance, or a wrist watch. In any event, the reference to bugs means that there is something wrong and the purchased item does not operate or function as expected.

Much of what we find on today's cluttered market is defective. Some of it is marked *imperfect* or *seconds* and placed on the bargain table. But far too much of what is bought has been produced on massive assembly lines under time pressure without adequate quality control for a commodity buying public that will not wait. Inspections are often hurried, so that each item is not carefully examined for flaws that could cause it to break or perform at less than peak output. In some instances, only every tenth or hundredth item is inspected at all in the presumption that those between will be acceptable. As a result, merchandise is returned in great quantities to merchants with the commonplace complaint that it will not work. The customer is usually irritated with the store manager, the manager with the manufacturer, the manufacturer with the labor force for shoddy workmanship, and the labor union with the factory management for bad working conditions and too little pay. So it is an aggravating situation all the way around.

Occasionally we find a manufacturer who takes pride in his work and carefully checks everything that leaves his plant to make sure that it meets the highest possible standards of excellence. This is sometimes a small company with only a few employees, small enough for the owner-manager to give personal attention and supervision. Often it is a new company struggling to get into an overcrowded market. And the irony of it is that the production of marketable items, which really excel, costs the small business more than it can afford. It either cuts the quality of its products, therefore, or it is squeezed out by the large corporations and monopolies.

With God it is different. He is not in competition with anyone or anything. And He is under no compulsion to produce in a hurry. The mills of God grind slowly. The quality of His creations will not be reduced in order to get a corner on the market. Either we pass inspection or He keeps working on us. And the fact that we all have flaws in us that need to be corrected accounts for our day to day experience of being sanded, adjusted, and polished by our Lord. When Jeremiah went down to the potter's house (Jeremiah 18:1-11), he saw the skilled craftsman take a marred vessel, put it back on the potter's wheel, and remake it into a vessel of rare beauty. Then God made it clear to the prophet that this is what He wanted to do

70

with the nation of Israel—shape and correct it after His own design. And His pattern for the Church is similar to that revealed to Jeremiah for Israel: "Christ loved the Church and gave himself up for her, that he might sanctify her, having cleansed her by the washing of water with the word, that he might present the church to himself in splendor, without spot or wrinkle or any such thing, that she might be holy and without blemish" (Ephesians 5:25-27). God's ultimate plan for the Church and each individual member of it is that we may all come to full perfection on the morning of the resurrection.

For the man who is unregenerate, not born anew (John 3:3), the Holy Spirit is always at work sowing the seed of the gospel in his heart. Not until he experiences the new birth does he really begin to live. And it is after that initial beginning of Christian life that God begins to use His tools upon one to get the bugs out and produce the kind of being who reflects the high value which the divine Creator places upon His workmanship.

If the non-believer wonders what God is trying to do with Him, the answer is simple. He is wooing such a person in love, seeking him like a lost sheep, sowing truth in his heart. He is taking the initiative to resurrect him from a life of sin and despair. And if the believer should ask what the divine work upon him may be, the answer is again quite simple. He is working out the bugs, cleaning up his life, shaping him for service here and hereafter. He is getting us in shape for the rewards to which the faithful are entitled in the world to come.

Can there be any question about my little old classic Volkswagon's reaction to the radical procedure through which it passed during those days of restoration? If it were a conscious being with feelings, it would have questioned everything that was happening to it. Many of the rusty bolts snapped off as the pressure was applied. And the dents in the body were literally beaten out with a hammer with blow upon blow. Holes were drilled again and again through the skeletal frame and the body itself. Chemical solutions were applied to rusted areas to heal the abrasions and patch up the wounds. Sharp gouges and rough sandpaper were used mercilessly as if the ordeal would never end. If that little car could have talked to me, it would have screamed from the pain. It would have accused me of being cruel and without compassion. It would have questioned my humaneness. There would have been constant whining and complaining, loud accusations that what I was doing had no purpose other than to inflict pain. Not until the entire renovation was completed and the little auto stood proudly with its bright red coat and its gleaming chrome did a wide smile stretch from headlight to headlight. Only then did it understand that my intentions were all above reproach, that the end result was worth all the pain, and that there was a wonderful purpose in the whole mystifying process.

Detecting the Weaknesses

Everyone has his weak spots. Some are weaker than others. And some respond more easily and profitably to the disciplines of God than do others who seem never to overcome their bent toward a line of least resistance. For 40 years the children of Jacob wandered in the wilderness en route to the Promised Land. There was no reason the journey from Egypt to Canaan should have taken so long. Had the people been faithful to the God of Abraham, the struggle against the rigors of their new freedom would have been greatly reduced. But they were weak. Even after the harsh treatment received from the hand of Pharaoh, which should have toughened them for the coming eventualities, the people were still unable to cope with hardship.

In the wilderness they complained because there was no water. They accused Moses of leading them into a more burdensome and intolerable situation than had been their lot in Egypt. At least there was food in Pharaoh's land and it appeared that none was going to be available for such large numbers of people in the wilds where they were. Every day was filled with murmurings and complaints indicative of a lack of trust in the God who had delivered them from slavery and promised them a country. At the very moment when Jehovah was declaring the moral bases upon which the new nation would be constructed, the unbelieving Hebrews were building a golden calf to worship at the foot of Mount Sinai. So steeped were they in their proneness to disbelieve and find their own way in the world that God refused to permit their generation to enter the Promised Land. And this is why 40 years were needed to traverse the wilderness. It took that long to raise up a new generation of Hebrews who would be more responsive to the disciplines of the Lord than had been those who departed from the land of Egypt.

Obviously, "God turned and gave them over to worship the host of heaven" (Acts 7:42) because they were "stiff necked people, uncircumcised in heart and ears, resisting the Holy Spirit" (Acts 7:51). When it is beyond doubt to God that any man or nation will ever respond to His plan, the Eternal Spirit relinquishes that one to his own way. But not until that point is reached does this ever happen. God is patient and slow to depart from His efforts with anyone.

But it does happen and we have the Scriptures themselves to verify that fact. Hosea hears God say, "Ephraim is joined to idols, let him alone" (Hosea 4:17). Paul speaks of those whom "God gave up in the lusts of their hearts to impurity, to the dishonoring of their bodies among themselves, because they exchanged the truth about God for a lie and worshiped and served the creature rather than the Creator" (Romans 1:24-25). Three times in this first chapter of the letter to the Romans the apostle uses the expression "gave them up" (Romans 1:24, 26, 28).

The Creator detects man's weaknesses and seeks to correct them, but He knows when there is no further value in discipline. A case in point is found in the ancient Church, where a man and his wife desired the honor that came from sacrifice, like the honor Barnabas received, while they were lying to the Holy Spirit (Acts 5:1-11). Because of the uselessness of continued discipline to correct this life of hypocrisy, human existence was suddenly terminated for the pretending couple. God sees what we do not see. He is sovereign ,and He is right in what He does, whether or not we accept His decision. There was no chance that Ananias and Sapphira would ever change, and the Lord knew it.

One afternoon the phone rang and a nurse, who was caring for an ill woman, requested that I call on her patient. She explained that Sally (to protect the identity of the lady I have used a fictitious name) was insisting that she was dying and that she was going to hell. Several bits of information were given to me before the call was made. Sally was a very intelligent woman, holding a doctorate in science and having worked as a specialist in her field during her healthier days. She and her deceased husband were wealthy landowners, but they had few if any friends and had lived somewhat isolated from the rest of the community. Membership was registered in a local church where her interests had been negligible through the years. Her priest had been called in earlier with little response from Sally. Nurses who tended her complained of her ill-tempered, negative attitude; her ill-treatment of those who tried to help her; her uncooperative spirit; and her talk about going to hell. She also had made it clear that she did not want to talk to any preacher. With this information in my mental file, I got into my car and drove to Sally's house.

On the bed lay a frail woman with long, stringy hair and eyes that were no more that mucous-filled slits. Fortunately, her mind appeared to be intact enough that she could understand what was being said to her. Assuring her that my visit was in no way to be considered an invasion of her privacy and that its purpose was solely to help her if she wished to be helped, the session was under way.

When asked whether she was a Christian, she quickly indicated that she was not. When asked if she wanted to be, her reply was a decisive no. As quietly and graciously as I knew how, I explained in simple terms what Christ had done for her and how she could become a Christian by confessing her sin and trusting in Him to deliver her from the despair that was heavy in the room. When asked if she would give her life to Jesus as her Savior, she made it clear that she would not. Then the one-sided conversation turned in a different direction. Explaining to her that the nurses had told me that she knew she was dying and was going to hell and that this was what she wanted, I gently asked if that were true. She said that it was. With all the compassion and love my heart felt at that moment, I passionately pleaded with her, explaining that she did not have to go to hell, that God would forgive her. But it was all for naught. A few days later Sally died.

Here was a woman who had lived her life without God. There is no way of knowing how many times the Lord had crossed her path and sought to draw her unto Himself. Apparently, there had never been any desire to know the Lord. If there had been, it did not show through in her dying hours. This was a perfect illustration of a person who had reached the point where God had given up on her, permitted her to die and find her own place. God never sends anyone to hell. We go to hell only when we choose to do so. And we choose to do so when we leave God out of our lives.

When our weaknesses are pointed out to us by the Holy Spirit, we are wise to cooperate with Him in allowing God to use His tools upon us. The disciples had their weaknesses as well as we, but the Lord knew that there was a chance for success with all of them except Judas Iscariot. Often God chastened and rebuked Simon Peter (Mark 8:33, 14:30, Matthew 26:52, Luke 9:35-36). James and John needed special attention, and apparently accepted it (Mark 9:39, 10:38). In fact, every man on the Lord's team was subjected to rigid correction (Luke 9:55), because He who knows our hearts saw what was askew in each of them. To live in this world is to have our personal imperfections revealed to us and to respond to the divine plan to refine us. This does not imply that we shall ever become perfect in this life, but it does mean that a readiness to become precisely what He desires should be our consuming passion.

One of the great self-trained men of God in the early twentieth century was Bud Robinson. In a sermon built around the healing of the blind man (Mark 8:22-26) called

"The Two Touches," Uncle Buddy (as he was affectionately referred to by all who knew him) tells how the Lord worked upon his own life. In his quaint manner, he says God began to "skim off" those attitudes from his heart that deterred him in living the Christian life. After enumerating a list of things the Lord was successfully taking from him, Uncle Buddy remarks, "I thought I was going to skimmings." Such a divine refinement of our lives is usually a severe and rigorous discipline, but it is a part of God's way of fitting us for purposeful citizenship in both worlds.

Better to Know It Now

If there is anything within us that militates against God's plan for us and His Kingdom, now is the time to find out about it. All through the Bible we are cautioned against shutting our eyes and ears to divine confrontations. "He who is often reproved, yet stiffens his neck, will suddenly be broken beyond healing" (Proverbs 29:1 RSV). Those are stern words. Reproof and correction are meant to effect changes in time and before it is too late. One can still be healed if he accepts reproof, but someday it will no longer be possible.

Jesus warned about the folly of building in defiance of the lack of a solid foundation. Such a man builds on sand and his house will come tumbling down in the coming storm. Only the one who builds on rock can expect to stand for all eternity (Matthew 7:24-27). These years are given to us in order that we may build a life that will be tested at the coming judgment (either the judgment against unbelief or the judgment of rewards). Paul refers to this latter judgment of rewards when "the fire shall test every man's work of what sort it is. If any man's work abide which he hath built upon it, he shall receive a reward. If any man's work shall be burned, he shall suffer loss; but he himself shall be saved, yet as by fire" (1 Corinthians 3:13-15). He speaks here of the construction of the building after the foundation is laid, that is, the works of the Christian life. Jesus, in the parable of the two builders, had in mind the laying of the foundation itself, which determines whether one must face a final judgment of doom. And the foundation? Nothing could be clearer than the words of the apostle, "No other foundation can anyone lay than that which is laid, which is Jesus Christ" (1 Corinthians 3:11 RSV).

A lifetime should be adequate for any man to make the foundation sure. At any moment during that life span we may turn in repentance and faith to Jesus as Savior and the foundation will be secured. We are also given a lifetime to choose the best available building materials out of which to construct a Christian life. This is the trial run and we are not to be given another chance once this earthly existence comes to an end. There is more beyond—much more—but the nature and quality of it depend on what we have done about the Lord Jesus Christ as Savior and how we have applied ourselves as disciples in the task of working out our salvation (Philippians 2:12). That is what is meant when we claim to know Christ as Lord, not only as Savior.

Knowing now where we are failing to grow and develop in Christian graces can spare us the disappointment of being *barely* saved. Everyone who finally reaches the heavenly city will be admitted solely on the merits of the crucified and risen Lord. Only they who have believed on the Lord Jesus Christ will find the gates opened to them. Nothing man can do will give him any claim to the land that is fairer than day. The level of that blessedness, however, will depend on the response which we have given to the leadership of the Holy Spirit and the degree of service rendered.

Some argue that they will be pleased as punch if they can just get inside the door. And it is true that our acceptance is all of grace. But it is also true that God must be more than displeased with any of us who plead the grace of the Lord as an excuse for lack of service and absence of development. If one ever recognizes the awful price which Christ paid for his salvation, he will never question the debt which he owes. Should we live to be a thousand years old, none of us could ever serve Him faithfully enough to deserve entrance into heaven. But because of what He has done for us, we give wholeheartedly of ourselves.

Qualifying in the Pre-trials

Those who enjoy auto racing find the qualifying trials almost as exciting as the race itself. The smell of rubber and gasoline, the screaming tires, and the screens of smoke are evidence that something exciting is going on. Every driver of an entry has his eye on the trophy, and he is willing to risk life and limb plus exorbitant amounts of money to make his dream come true. Expectancy fills the air, and the loud shouting above the roar of the engines only adds to the excitement.

No car is allowed in the race until it qualifies. And there is more to it than just attaining a pre-determined distance in a specified time. Speed is not the whole of it. Both the car and the driver must be checked out to be certain that there is no deception, that everything is in order for honest competition. The owner is meticulous about making sure that the car is safe, all mechanical parts are working perfectly, and the driver is in the best possible condition both physically and emotionally. Only as certain checkpoints are passed is the car entered in the forthcoming race.

The whole thing is a kind of illustration of life itself. Getting into the race is the first concern. All around us are people who have never entered the race. From all appearances they are not even remotely interested in qualifying. They just exist, and their lives are not very exciting. To be perfectly honest, it is all a bit boring. Not until man is moved by the Holy Spirit and responds to His motivation does he begin to qualify for life's race. Prior to that time we are literally out of it. And it is precisely at the moment when we accept the Lord Jesus Christ as personal Savior that the checkpoints are passed.

Once a man has qualified for the race, he is in position to do the best driving he can. Living the Christian life is done in the same manner. We must give it all we have got! Being in the race is an honor in itself. God has made it all possible. And every man who is not disqualified on his disbelief is a winner on his commitment and service. He is in the race, but there are several degrees of reward. And no man is properly motivated who runs for the prize as an end in itself. The desire to place is for the glory of Him who has given us the right to be in the running at all. We will have more to say about rewards in a later chapter.

Nothing But the Best

God wants only the best of men. Not that He accepts only the best, but rather that He accepts even the very bad who believe and then sets Himself to the business of making us into the best we can become. For this reason, our performance in this world as followers of Christ is vitally important. We owe our lives to our Redeemer. Hence, there is no reason for any Christian to be satisfied with his present level of attainment. The apostle Paul spoke directly to this truth long ago in his letter to the church at Philippi: "Not that I have already obtained this [he had been speaking of the desire to share with Christ in the resurrection of the dead in the world to come] or am already perfect; but I press on to make it my own, because Christ Jesus has made me his own . . . I press on toward the goal for the prize of the upward call of God in Christ Jesus" (Philippians 3:12-14 RSV).

Not many of us are as zealous to reach the highest goal of all. We are satisfied to be saved by the skin of our teeth. Escaping hell fire and damnation is about the extent of it for some people. How like us it is to go through life without using all of our cylinders. We allow ourselves to be sluggish rather than put ourselves at the disposal of God for a tune-up which would give us new impetus and needed thrust.

Serving faithfully in Jesus' name is man's way of sharing the mission of Christ to the world. The world needs the witness and service of every Christian. Yet it may be that the Christian needs the benefits of growth and development which such action brings even more than does the neighbor to whom he goes. In some strange and mystic way man is saved as he saves others. Is this not what the Master meant when He said, "Whoever would save his life will lose it; and whoever loses his life for my sake and the gospel's will save it"? (Mark 8:35 RSV).

The best of men are those who burn themselves out in discipleship. Far too many of us rust out and have nothing left to present to the Master when He comes. What a shame to waste these priceless years in inactivity when so much needs to be done in the world about us and so much more needs to be accomplished in the refinement of our own souls! How well I remember the challenge of a gospel song from the earlier days of my walk with God, words that hauntingly come back to me again and again in the quiet of the night. The refrain of this soul inspiring song should motivate us all.

> Let me burn out for Thee, dear Lord,
> Burn and wear out for Thee.
> Don't let me rust or my life be
> A failure my God to Thee.
> Use me and all I have, dear Lord,
> And get me so close to Thee,
> That I feel the throb
> Of the great heart of God.
> And let me burn out for Thee.

Life may be "an empty dream" for some, including Robert Browning, but it is far more than that for the man or woman who is alert to the plan of God in every life and the overall design of the Creator for His creation. Some of us need to stop dreaming and wake up to the glorious end which the Lord has arranged for us and to the exciting means for achieving it, which He has provided.

In Readiness
No one can read very far into the New Testament until he is face to face with the injunction to preparedness. The Lord Himself told a story about a wedding where some of the bridesmaids were not prepared for the happy occasion.

Thus, they were left outside the festivities of the nuptial celebration (Matthew 25:1-13). There is little question but that the incident was a warning related directly to the Second Coming of Christ. But the parable has overtones of alarm that make it applicable to all of life and the numerous exigencies with which man is confronted daily. At the conclusion of His parable of the householder who failed to be on guard and was robbed by a house breaker, the Lord added, "Therefore you also must be ready; for the Son of man is coming at an hour you do not expect" (Matthew 24:44 RSV). This was also a warning to be prepared for the return of our Master in power and judgment, but the overtones of imminent alarm are there as well.

The tenor of the Christian Scriptures is one of expectancy. We are urged to be in readiness all the time for whatever may happen in the next moment. No man needs to be caught unprepared if he understands that this life has been given to us primarily for that reason. Whether it is the return of Christ for His Church or our own physical death, let every man live every day in readiness for an appearance before the King. Let Paul be our example who, when the people begged him not to go to Jerusalem for fear that he would be jailed, affirmed, "I am ready not only to be imprisoned but even to die at Jerusalem for the name of the Lord Jesus" (Acts 21:13 RSV). And when the hour of his martyrdom approached, Paul could write to young Timothy, "I am already on the point of being sacrificed; the time of my departure has come. I have fought the good fight, I have finished the race, I have kept the faith; henceforth there is laid up for me a crown of righteousness, which the Lord, the righteous judge, shall give me at that day; and not to me only, but unto all them also that love his appearing" (2 Timothy 4:6-8 RSV). No sadness or dejection is detected in his voice. He was ready!

These days constitute a trial run. Not everyone will be ready when the day of judgment comes. Some will. He who has received Christ by faith will be in readiness for life in the next world. And he who has dedicated his days and energies to serving the Lord who has saved him will be prepared for the promised rewards as well. Only the man or woman who does not waste this life can be in readiness for the amplified one reserved for us in Christ when the new day dawns.

She was very young. The cancer was advanced before there was any sign of being ill. Within a few weeks that beautiful lady wasted away, and what had been a robust and healthy mother was gone. A few days before she died she was heard to exclaim in a clear voice, as if she had been suddenly surprised, "O, my beautiful home! My beautiful home!" The earthly home where she lived with her minister husband and three children was comfortable but ordinary. In no way could it ever be described as surprisingly beautiful. Without a doubt, she was seeing something she had never seen before. Did not Jesus say something about "many mansions"? Well, we all know where they are. And we know where she is. She was my wife.

— Chapter 5 —

The Rigors of Prepration

Anticipating the Journey

Foolish beyond belief is the man who knows that he will soon have to make a long and arduous trip, yet never concerns himself about making the needed arrangements. Normally such a person would begin long before the departure date to make careful plans for each important detail. Maps would be procured and studied. Expenses likely to be incurred would be considered. Comparison between available methods of travel and types of accommodations would be of utmost importance. If the trip happened to be one which would take him out of the country, such a traveler would get a medical check up including a series of inoculations against illness, apply for a passport, and investigate as thoroughly as possible what risks might be involved. No one but a fool would walk blindly unprepared into either a business or a pleasure trip without first having thought the matter through and having taken steps to get ready.

The average person on the street would be hard-pressed to come up with an answer should he be asked, "If you should die tonight, do you know that you would go to heaven"? If he should finally come up with something like, "Well, I think so," the next question would be, "Do you have your grips packed"? Pretty simple, isn't it?

Living in this interval of time alone requires a great deal of care and planning. Jesus observed that no man "desiring to build a tower, does not first sit down and count the cost, whether he has enough to complete it" (Luke 14:28 RSV). The analogy was specifically related to the cost of discipleship, but its underlying truth is pertinent to all of life. Yet, anticipating a journey that will move one from the known world into an unexplored realm from which no traveler ever returns makes planning for life's little day on earth pale into insignificance. To be aware that earthly life will one day end in a mound of earth quiet and still, and yet do nothing about the possibility of something more to follow, is an incredibly immature way to live.

A valet, who had worked for a businessman and his wife for most of his life, overheard well meaning friends at the mortuary discussing the sudden death of the head of the house. Someone was piously surmising that the deceased had just taken another of his frequent trips, this time into the wonderful city of God. But the valet was not so sure. To his own circle of friends he confided that every other trip taken by his employer had involved a good bit of preparation. But, to his knowledge, he had never seen him do anything or even heard him say anything that made it appear that he was getting ready for the journey of death. And such a journey just does not take care of itself.

Logic alone would demand that if we anticipate and get ready for earth's little trips, we should likewise be prepared for the big one reserved for the end. Surely there is something wrong when a person takes more time and effort getting ready to spend a two-week vacation than he gives to planning how and where he will spend eternity. Eternity is a long time—much too long—to be careless about. It is the nature of all of us, however, to ignore the inevitable until we are forced to face it.

Being Acclimated to the Beyond

Space travel is still in its infancy. Already some amazing feats have been performed by scientists, technicians, engineers, and astronauts. Just a few brief years ago no one but Buck Rogers and a few other visionaries dared to dream of traveling to the moon and back. Space fiction was interesting because it was stimulating for man's adventurous spirit. But it was all a contribution to man's entertainment, certainly not to his discussions of reality. Today's gift to history includes unbelievable investigations of space and offers previews of inter-planetary travel which will take earthlings to the most distant reaches of our telescopes and beyond.

A special and rare breed of humanity is demanded for the task of making these space flights. Not everyone could do it. Frankly, of those who could, only a few would! The flight itself is rigorous enough, but it is the torturous training through which an astronaut must pass that tells the kind of stuff he is made of.

Candidates for space travel must submit to numerous physical, psychological, and emotional tests before being subjected to the training program. Once the grueling examinations are passed, the astronaut enters a world of unbelievable conditioning. The conditions under which he lives are as similar to those found in outer space as is humanly possible to reproduce. He must learn to navigate himself as well as his ship in a strange world where the gravitational pull is reduced to nothing. At the other extreme, the astronaut in training has to learn how to cope with the excessive speed of the rocket that pushes him beyond the pull of the earth. In a matter of minutes he moves from a state of enormous gravitational pull to one of almost none at all. As lay people, who live outside the arena of space technology, all of this discussion is nearly unintelligible.

Added to the necessity of learning to handle gravity, the astronaut must also be able to accept the unexpected without panic. The last thing he can afford to do is lose his cool. That would be disastrous. His eating habits are completely altered, moveable space within the ship is at a premium, and the aloneness is far from easy even when there are colleagues sharing the endeavor. Even we who do not engage in such rigorous training are sensitive to what must be an uncanny period of acclimatization.

So difficult is the training of a Christian for his coming confrontation with the beyond that Christ has given us specific instruction with a warning: "Enter by the narrow gate; for the gate is wide and the way is easy, that leads to destruction, and those who enter by it are many. For the gate is narrow and the way is hard, that leads to life, and those who find it are few" (Matthew 7:13-14 RSV). As is the case with the astronauts, so is the case with Christians—there are not many of them, because the disciplines of becoming acclimated to the life to come are so very demanding. The rigors of Christian discipleship were further clarified in the Master's words to the multitude: "If any man would come after me, let him deny himself and take up his cross and follow me" (Mark 8:34 RSV). Self-denial, cross bearing, and imitation of

Christ—it all smacks of a very rigorous and demanding life which too few are willing to pursue.

Excesses in Asceticism

Extremism is a formidable foe, against which every deeply committed Christian must do battle. Once we have decided to pursue that way of self-denial and cross bearing, we must carefully delineate between the disciplines that are constructive and those which are actually useless and sometimes harmful. In their dedication to the law of Moses, the Pharisees of Jesus' day were desecrating a holy discipline with excesses that rendered the divine mandate into a systematized life of misery and hypocrisy. The Ten Commandments had been multiplied by 60 until the resultant moral code was an intolerable burden which fractured the spirit and left Judaism a crippled nation. Nothing incensed the Son of God more than religious extremism which made a mockery of God's will for His people.

To the troubled church at Corinth the apostle Paul wrote, "Every athlete exercises self control in all things. They do it to receive a perishable wreath, but we an imperishable. Well, I do not run aimlessly. I do not box as one beating the air; but I pommel my body and subdue it, lest after preaching to others, I myself should be disqualified" (1 Corinthians 9:25-26 RSV). The Scriptures do not require, nor do they condone, physical abuse, but they do insist on discipline of both mind and body. In the Galatian letter self-control is included among the eight by-products of the fruit of the Spirit, which is love (Galatians 5:22-23). But there is a considerable difference between self- discipline and self destruction. The apostle to the Gentiles sought to bring himself into subjection to the divine goals for him, but he did not run aimlessly or box as one beating the air. That is, there was a definite purpose in what he did, a specific and desired end in view. Much of what the Pharisees were doing was so perfunctorily done that the reason had been buried and forgotten. In reality, their keeping of the law in such meticulous manner was not a means to a divine consummation, but it was an end in itself.

Cloistered behind monastery walls, the monks often fell heir to the same kind of excesses. Martin Luther tells of the abuse he gave his body during those harrowing days of his monkery. Charity, sobriety, chastity, and poverty were only the beginning in his practice of the counsels of perfection. Literal mortification of the flesh was a daily objective. Even the blankets allowed him in his cubicle were deliberately cast aside in an effort to freeze himself to death during the long winter nights. Luther admitted that he nearly killed himself with the rigors of monastic life. Yet, he failed to find peace and became more and more disenchanted with living as the austerities increased. How miserable he was. And how deep-seated was his hatred of the God who would not be satisfied.

Among us today are to be found some well-intentioned people who nevertheless succumb to a life of useless and often harmful asceticism. In their presence we are reminded of the man for whom the physician prescribed one pill per day, but who took ten in the belief that if one pill would help, ten pills would help him ten times as much! When one's religion takes all the fun out of life, he had better take a long, hard look at its validity. Did not our Lord say, "I am come that they might have life, and have it abundantly" (John 10:10 RSV). Joy is a distinguishing mark of the true Christian. A doleful churchman is far from being a good advertisement for Christianity. What the Lord wants is not pretentious fanaticism, but disciplined radiance.

Before going any further in our discussion of asceticism, we need to remind ourselves that extreme forms of discipline, while counterproductive, are not a problem for most of us. Our problem lies in the almost total lack of discipline at all. Permissiveness has become a way of life, and it has been adopted and blessed by the church. For this reason, it is a rarity today to see any man or woman who is more than superficially concerned with what used to be called holy habits. Christians are soft and pampered, spiritually pudgy and short-winded. We are terribly out of shape. Needed as much as anything else is a spiritual health program by which the man or woman in training can develop muscle and tone up the spirit. The following sections in this chapter will offer some suggestions as to how one might go about this program without going to demoralizing extremes.

The Calisthenics of Prayer

Christ was an expert in prayer. Because of His adeptness at communicating with the Father in heaven, the disciples asked that He instruct them. His formal instruction consisted of the model prayer recorded in Matthew 6:9-13. There were other occasions when Jesus, in a more informal manner, sought to leave an indelible impression about the need for prayer. An example is the parable of the widow who refused to be defeated and persisted until the judge came to her aid (Luke 18:1-8). Luke suggests that the reason the parable was told to the disciples was to enforce the fact "that they ought always to pray and not lose heart". It is probably true that prayer is needed more when it is harder to do than at any other time. When it is difficult to jog in the morning or do a half-dozen push ups before breakfast, we know how out of shape we are and how much we need the workout. So it is with prayer in the life of a believer.

Entire nights were often devoted to prayer by the Lord. Under the night stars, in solitude, on the Mount of Olives, the Savior toned His spirit. It would have been much easier to sleep—and a great deal more comfortable. But the requirements for the mission for which He came into the world were so stiff that He had to keep Himself in shape for the conflicts He met day after day. Marcus Aurelius was correct when he defined life as a battle. For some it seems to be a losing battle, but not for Jesus. Not even on Calvary! The battle had been won inch by inch, day by day in a disciplined life of prayer. In the Garden of Gethsemane, the final amen was said and the conquest assured. Christ would win in death. What a grand insight. Unless man wins in that hour, all the earlier victories will have been fought for naught. He who lives in daily communion with God through prayer will not have that communion broken by so insignificant a thing as physical death.

Prayer expands one's mind, sensitizes his soul, braces him for life's exigencies, and keeps him in tune with the Creator's design. A vital aspect of the earliest Christian community was the prominent place devoted to both private and public prayer. Together the struggling fellowship raised their voices in praise and petition. Nothing was too big to challenge God with and nothing was so small as to be unworthy of His attention. All of life was lived in open partnership with the Lord. Throughout the succeeding history of the Christian Church every great movement of lasting value has been launched in prayer and all who deserve the honor of being among the saints have been warriors whose major weapon was prayer.

Everyone ought to set aside a time and place for prayer. Without daily devotions one becomes spiritually sluggish, run down, and easily defeated. When one's days become too complicated for prayer, they are far too cluttered for any kind of emotional health. Man was made for communion with His Maker and he must establish priorities which do not crowd out that communion. The rigorous discipline of prayer is far less difficult than the rigorous consequences of prayerlessness. One point of caution , however, needs to be made here. It would be a mistake to think that one is living a life of prayer just because a time and place is set apart daily for such exercise. Prayer is not the articulating of words nor is it a scheduled routine which can become a limiting factor. Rather prayer is a lifestyle which characterizes one's existence twenty-four hours a day. It is essentially friendship with God, a frame of mind, a disposition of soul, an intimate communal relationship with the living Lord. That is what is meant by praying without ceasing. This kind of praying goes on while we work and play, even when we sleep. To be conscious of the presence of the Lord and amenable to whatever that presence dictates, is prayer at its very best.

Exercising through Fasting

No Christian discipline endorsed in the New Testament is more neglected than fasting. It is never mentioned in church, no sermons are devoted to it, church school curriculum refuses to get entangled by it, and the whole idea is foreign to a society where overeating is commonplace. Let none make the mistake, however, of equating fasting with dieting. Half of the American population is in the habit of dieting at least occasionally to keep physically trim. Such a procedure has little or no spiritual value since the desired end has nothing to do with one's faith. Fasting is as beneficial to the underweight person as to him who is obese since its objective is to concentrate on spiritual growth.

Fasting, like any other means of preparation for living here and hereafter, can be an empty facade. That is exactly what it was for the leaders of the religious world in Jesus' day. Their entire life, including both prayer and fasting, was one of pretending to be holy on the basis of outward manifestations. This is why they fasted twice a week rather than just on the Day of Atonement once a year as the Law specified. By overdoing it, there was created a deceptive sense of *extra* holiness. And when they did so Jesus pointed out that they "disfigure their faces" (Matthew 6:16) so that others would know the sacrifice which they had made. Needless to say, they had in the acclaim of men all the reward they would ever get. Though these religionists may not have been conscious of it, that was the extent of what they really wanted. The end had been achieved.

When the disciples had failed in their attempt to heal a young boy brought to them by his father, our Lord proceeded to do what His men had been incapable of accomplishing. At once the disciples knew that Jesus was disappointed with them. In response to their question as to why they had so miserably failed, the Master explained that such power as He had displayed was produced only "by prayer and fasting" (Matthew 17:21). If there had been no other word from the Lord about the value of fasting, we would all recognize its importance on the basis of this gentle rebuke alone.

On one occasion the concerned Twelve insisted that Jesus had spent enough time in devotion and service, that He should at least take time to refresh Himself with food. His reply was most interesting and enlightening: "I have meat to eat that you know not of" (John 4:32). Indeed, there is available for those who would fast and pray a supply of heavenly nourishment without which the spirit of man shrivels and dies. Malnutrition of the soul could be so easily avoided if we spent as much time and effort in feeding the spirit as we do in nourishing and stuffing the body. Fasting not only indicates to God our seriousness in the concern that He has clearly laid out, but it clears our own perception so that we can more directly concentrate on the matter. May it not be that the Lord is unhappy with His followers who lavish so much on the physical demands of the flesh and allow the spiritual cries to go unheeded? We have a long way to go here before a proper balance is achieved.

A Workout in Biblical Studies

Neglect of the written Word of God is more costly than any of us can afford. There is absolutely no excuse for ignorance about the contents of the Bible. Anyone who desires to know the message of God to man as preserved in the Scriptures can find a church somewhere in his area where the Bible is honored and preached. In the unlikely event that no such organization of the institutional church can be located, there is bound to be a neighborhood group of Christians meeting in someone's home. In addition, Bible helps of all kinds are available in bookstores, and classes are usually found in Bible schools and seminaries in the larger cities.

God would not have given His Word and shared His plan for the ages unless He intended for man to study and obey it. Why would He have moved sensitive men to write down the divine truth if it were not to be read and examined by men and women in every age to come? Many uses can be found for the Scriptures, and none of them should be neglected. Paul reminds Timothy of this: "All scripture is inspired of God and profitable for teaching, for reproof, for correction, and for training in righteousness, that the man of God may be complete, equipped for every good work" (2 Timothy 3:16-17 RSV). Earlier in this same letter the writer warns against useless speculation and disputes. Only one way is known by which a man can insure himself against a false view of life. Therefore, both Timothy and we are admonished, "Do your best to present yourself to God as one approved, a workman who has no need to be ashamed, rightly handling the word of truth" (2 Timothy 2:15 RSV).

Just to read the Bible is not enough. In fact, Bible reading can be a waste of time unless the reader understands what he is reading. For this reason, Bible reading should be planned at a time when there is no reason to be hurried and in a place where no one except others who are studying will be apt to disturb. Never should we leave a passage until every honest attempt has been made to understand it. Sometime this may demand a return to the same passage several study periods in a row. It is unfair to claim that one does not understand the Bible when he has spent less time with it than with the morning newspaper or the evening television schedule. One of life's most exciting and valuable work-outs is to be discovered in a systematic and persevering study of the written Word of God.

Gymnastics of Sanctity

Abstention from attitudes and activities that would make our integrity suspect is not to be denied. Certainly, life is not best perceived as a series of negatives. But, on the other hand, every positive approach presupposes a negative. As with almost everything, there needs to be a balance between the positive and the negative. Being Christlike is basically a positive thing, but it requires some resistance also. The first letter to the church at Thessalonica draws to a close with the injunction to "abstain from every form of evil" (1 Thessalonians 5:22 RSV).

Since the very beginning of the covenant—actually since the creation of man—some ways of living have not been open to him who would be God-like. Adam was forbidden to eat of the tree of the knowledge of good and evil (Genesis 2:17). Moses was given ten laws from Jehovah which were four-fifths negative (Exodus 20:1-17). In the Sermon on the Mount, where Jesus heightens the laws of the older Jewish community, our Lord is not afraid to forbid specific attitudes and actions which are foreign to the way of Christ. Clearly, He is not setting up a new law to replace the Mosaic covenant, but He is making it clear that not every kind of action or thought is acceptable to God and that all of us are guilty.

While no one wants or needs to give the impression of being pious or sanctimonious, a Christian cannot live just any old way the world about him lives. Only by being different, by having higher moral standards, stronger ethical values, and firmer convictions does the believer influence the unbeliever. A Christian must take care what he does, where he goes, with whom he continually associates, and even how he permits himself to think. This does not mean that anyone needs to be a prude, but it does mean that every child of God must remember *whose* he is and live so as not to disgrace or even reflect upon His Lord. For the born-again believer, such admonition should be hardly necessary. The legitimate Christian has a new nature that insists upon sanctity about which we will have more to say as a way of life when temptation is evaluated in a later chapter.

Flexing the Muscles through Service

Legislation by federal and state government is a poor method of carrying out the will of God in service to our fellow man. In a society where most men and women are unregenerate and all are sinners, the need for such legislation is obvious. But it is still a poor substitute. Pronouncements by denominational boards and agencies are of little value in the practical outworking of Christian service. Hardly anyone pays much attention to what either a hierarchy or the bureaucrats of the church have to say. It goes in one ear and out the other without so much as disturbing the gray matter between them. Government legislation and ecclesiastical pronouncements are poor excuses for the kind of person to person service given by the good Samaritan to the beaten Jewish traveler in the moving story as told by our Lord (Luke 16:19-31).

Bud Wilkinson, football coach of national fame, was once asked by a reporter what he thought the game of football contributes to physical fitness. His unexpected answer was, "Absolutely nothing!" Asked to explain what he meant, the coach said, "I define football as twenty-two men on the field desperately needing rest and forty-thousand people in the stands desperately needing exercise." For a long time church people have acted as though preachers, missionaries, and social workers are employed by the church to play the game of service while the rest of us sit in the pews as spectators. Lately the laity has begun to get into the game, too. And we are finding out that the contribution of the Church to spiritual fitness can be of inestimable strength when we stop over taxing a few while the sluggish masses just sit and cheer or boo, depending on whether the few are playing the game to suit them.

Witness As a Means of Shaping Up

No one who has even a surface knowledge of the history of evangelism and mission can ever forget the name of John R. Mott. Young people especially were turned on for the work of witnessing to the whole world by this Christian layman who rejected both the presidency of Princeton University and the position of Secretary of State because he believed there was something greater that he was called to do. He used to say, "If a man has religion, he must do one of two things with it; if it is false, he must give it up; if it is true, he must give it away".

Some people who claim to be Christians appear ill at ease when the conversation turns toward Christ. As long as religious talk skirts the main issue, they communicate. But once it moves in the direction of personal contact with a living Lord and Savior, the communication channels get clogged. Such persons are embarrassed as though the Lord were too private and sacred to be shared. Could anything be more out of place in the life of a Christian than timidity or embarrassment in the midst of an opportunity to witness to His redeeming grace? Has not Jesus warned us, "Whoever is ashamed of me and my words in this adulterous and sinful generation, of him will the Son of man also be ashamed, when he comes in the glory of the Father with the holy angels" (Mark 8:38).

Sojourning on this earth gives us all an excellent chance to make our lives square with our words. Each of us knows some who talk piously but without living so as to back up their words. That is hypocrisy pure and simple. Let no one pretend to be religious. On the other hand, "Let the redeemed of the Lord say so!" (Psalm 107:2). True witnessing has nothing to do with pretense, since the witness is never to one's own goodness but to the grace and mercy of God who has condescended to save us. In a real way, witnessing is bragging on Jesus.

Nothing more deeply enriches a believer's days than to become involved in witnessing for Christ to others. One grows as he shares. By the same token, he shrinks if he hoards what has been given to him. Either discipleship will destroy secrecy or secrecy will destroy discipleship. And either we become vocal about Jesus Christ or we lose Him. Stagnation and death, like that which characterizes the Dead Sea, come to any person who receives the grace of God and dams up the flow into the lives of those who dwell around him. Witnessing here is preparation for that day when "every tongue will confess" (Romans 14:11) and all will declare, "Blessing, and honor, and glory, and power, be unto him that sitteth upon the throne, and unto the Lamb forever and ever" (Revelation 5:13). None will be able to join that worshiping and witnessing throng of the redeemed in the world to come who has not learned to open his lips in praise and testimony while here on the earth. There are so many ways to witness, to give one's faith away. In addition to direct verbal communication, one may give free reading material which will present the cause of Christ. Buy a good book and give it to a friend to read. He may never pick it up, but then he may out of curiosity start reading and end up being a believer. Be creative. Ask God to show you the best way to entice a neighbor to think about his need of Christ.

— Chapter 6 —

The Meaning of Temptation

A Plot As Old As Man Himself

In order that we may not miss the integral place temptation is to have in the earthly pilgrimage of man, the subject is bluntly introduced to us on the opening pages of the Bible. And it is doubly significant to observe that the first couple in the garden was subjected to temptation before anything else transpired in their brand new world. Before they had hardly dried from creation, the newly made pair was confronted by a subtle creature whose intent was to mold their soft wills into something different from what the Creator had designed. The serpent probably walked erect (Genesis 3:14) before the Fall and was capable of communication with man (Genesis 3:1-5). It is reasonable to assume that Satan simply utilized the form of the serpent, as he later demonized individuals in New Testament times and literally spoke through them, in order to speak to and seduce Eve.

Throughout the Old Testament the insidious work of Satan is seen again and again. Other than the creation story, the most classic illustration of the use of temptation is found in the poetic book of Job. There a righteous man is nearly destroyed by the vicious attacks of Satan in an effort to prove that all religion is embraced by selfish reasons. It was the objective of the Tempter to verify his theory that men serve God only for what they get out of it. A lengthy discourse would be in order here on Job and his trials, but we will reserve further remarks for the section on suffering and its use in the human test.

Since the beginning, man has been caught between God and Satan. Both seek to mold and shape the human creature, and it is man's choice who tips the balance one way or the other. With Adam, the choice brought disaster, as is always true when we succumb to the deceptive promises of Satan. With Job, the choice brought blessing and reward. The difference did not lie in one's being better by nature than the other. It lay, rather, in Job's determination to remain faithful to his Creator and Sustainer.

Never in the history of the human race has anyone lived upon the earth who was free from temptation. We do not hear much warning against it in church anymore, but it is the lot of every man. Of course, the degree of temptation varies with the individual. The less rigid and more flexible one is in his convictions about compromise, the lighter will seem his battle with the Tempter. Inevitably, as one lives in closer relationship with God, his temptations increase. Furthermore, as the Christian resists the Tempter the fierceness of Satan's will to win magnifies the role of temptation into giant proportions of monstrous evil.

Temptation in the Life of Christ

At the very outset of our analysis, it must be established beyond doubt that being tempted is not synonymous with sinning. Otherwise, our Lord who was "without sin" (Hebrews 4:15) was as sinful as any other. Jesus' ordeal with Satan came at the commencement of His public ministry even as Adam's began at the genesis of his servanthood in the garden of Eden. Christ is called by Paul "the last Adam" (1 Corinthians 15:45), which means that a new humanity is born in Him. What the first Adam did in bringing down upon mankind the curse of sin, the second *undid* in bringing down to man the grace of God. Temptation, however, was as much a part of the new humanity as it had been a part of the old. The response of Jesus was so vastly different from that of Adam that those persons related to the "second Adam from heaven" (1 Corinthians 15:47) have an advantage over those related only to the father of the old humanity. Every man is tempted either in Adam or in Christ depending upon which of the two he is more intimately in union with at the time of the attack.

Three attempts were made by Satan to deter the Lord from His sinless life and divine mission. First, there was the invitation to surrender to an obsession with the gratification of fleshly appetite. Jesus was hungry after 40 days and nights of fasting, and the human appetite is legitimate. It is given to us by God. But it must never be permitted to become so important that all our powers are devoted to it. Man's flesh demands food, drink, sleep, and sex, but in each instance the appetite must be controlled, at times refused.

Second, there was the temptation to act in a spectacularly reckless manner while demanding God to protect Him. Presumption can be a grave sin. God is not obligated to defend or sustain us when we live in open defiance of the laws which govern human existence. When one lives in careless or rebellious ways and then blames God for the harm that comes to him, he has sinned. Jesus refused to take advantage of the love of the heavenly Father.

Third, there was the temptation to believe that He could be whole in the service of the enemy of God. He was asked to surrender the whole of Himself to Satan, to be undivided in his allegiance. This is the complete and final temptation of them all, the Satanic offer, which, if accepted, proves one's undoing. To succumb to that seduction would have been to forfeit His union with God and to fail in His Messianic mission. It would have been to sin against the Holy Spirit and destroy the Father's plan of the ages.

The fact that both Adam and Jesus were subjected to severe sieges of temptation is a confirmation of the statement that no one is exempt. And it is illuminating to observe that the three categories of temptation to which our Lord was exposed cover the general range of human possibilities. All temptations can be classified under provision (physical gratification), protection (insurance against failure), or preeminence (worldly power and prestige). In light of this fact the writer of Hebrews could say of Jesus, "We have not a high priest who is unable to sympathize with our weaknesses, but one who in every respect has been tempted as we are, yet without sinning" (Hebrews 4:15 RSV). It is a big order, but keeping check on ourselves at these three crucial points of vulnerability, and overcoming the enticements to being less than what we are called upon to become, is a priority for believers. The path of least resistance is to fall in line with the demonic enemy and succumb to his deceptive tactics, which so persuasively convince us that what is being suggested to us will enhance our pleasure.

The Desire to Be Free from God

Built into every thought of sin is the conscious or unconscious wish to dispose of God. Our unredeemed egos demand their autonomous rights, their places of elevated self-rule. In every man's heart there is a struggle for supremacy. Intuitively we all know that the human heart houses both a cross and a throne. Either God is on the throne and man is on the cross of self-surrender or man is on the throne and God is on the cross. It has to be one way or the other. There is no alternative. Individually we have been entrusted with these years of earthly existence in order that the decision may be made as to who shall sit on the throne. And it is the nature of unregenerate humanity to do almost anything to keep from abdicating the throne.

Temptation in all its forms is appealing because through it we are offered a chance to be free of God. At least it seems that way. Ultimately no one can be free from the ever-present Spirit of the Creator. Long ago the psalmist recognized this to be the case as he penned the insightful words, "If I ascend to heaven, thou art there! If I make my bed in Sheol, thou art there!" (Psalm 139:8). Regardless of the folly in trying to free ourselves from Him who has created us and seeks to redeem our fallen spirits, masses of men and women continue to make the effort.

Adam was promised emancipation from a Creator who would make his existence unbearable if he did not break free from the divine shackles. Once the break was completed the man was assured that he would "be like God" (Genesis 3:5), that is to say that the creature would be in a position to compete with and annul responsibility to the Creator. Each succeeding seduction by Satan has been for the express purpose of alienating men from God into a pseudo freedom which provides a kind of false security in being our own Creator, Redeemer, and Judge.

Jealousy and Hatred for God

Traditionally, the origin of Satan is attributed to an uncontrollable jealousy toward the creating God by one of the created angels. The account of this story is found in Isaiah 14 and is referred to by Jesus in Luke 10:18. Being jealous of the sovereignty of the Creator, Lucifer (Satan's angelic name before the Fall) entered into conflict in heaven in hopes of usurping the divine throne for himself. The plot aborted, and he was cast down to the earth where he continues his war against the Lord of heaven and earth.

Jealousy has now given place to a venomous hatred for the deity who has defeated him. Being no longer in heaven and hence unable to get at God directly, Satan now pursues his evil plan in an indirect way. Man is tempted to do what Satan was unsuccessful in achieving. If the sworn enemy of God can turn the Lord's creation against Him, the original diabolic objective will have been accomplished. For this reason, we discover within our hearts the seeds of jealousy and hatred, which Satan cultivates and tries to bring to fruition. This is why one has little, if any, chance of resistance until he is in Christ (2 Corinthians 5:17). Temptation for the man in Christ can be overcome. For him who is still only in Adam, there is every reason to expect final surrender to the insistent suggestion of the Tempter.

Creating discord and chaos is the business of the fallen angel bent on disrupting the peaceful order willed by the Lord for His people. "God is not the God of confusion but of peace" (1 Corinthians 14:33). All the seething turmoil, restlessness, and existential meaninglessness so prevalent in the world is not the work of Jehovah. Satan is wholly responsible for it all. Strange as it may seem to us, however, the Lord permits temptation because it can ultimately serve His purpose as well as that of Satan. Temptation itself is neither good nor bad. It is amoral. The response of man determines its usefulness or devastating potential.

The Dual Role of Temptation

Humanity exists in a state of real tension. Everyone feels the pull of God, whose gracious will is to lift us into closer union with Himself. Beneath us is the tug of Satan, whose vicious will is to drag us down to an eventual separation from the Lord. We are caught in the middle between these two magnetic poles of attraction. But there is no hint of blind fate here or a game played between God and Satan, a game over which we have no control. It is man's decision which determines which of the two will be successful.

Even after man has made his decision to cast his vote for one or the other, there remains a healthy lifelong tension that survives as long as human life endures. Without the opposing pulls, we could drift off into some mystic, semi-spirit realm less than fully human or sink into some evil, demonic existence. The tension keeps us human and is not relaxed or withdrawn until death.

Satan's purpose in temptation, as has been noted, is to seduce us into rebellion and consummate destruction in hell. God's purpose is to try our spirits, to test us. The same temptation may fulfill either of these objectives. Only in a passive role is God involved in the attack upon man's integrity. Active aggression is solely the part of Satan, with the Lord permitting the test and offering reinforcement to the besieged citadel of the human heart.

James was dead certain that the Father in heaven has no active part in temptation. In the opening words of his epistle he writes, "Let no one say when he is tempted, I am tempted by God, for God cannot be tempted with evil and he himself tempts no one" (James 1:13 RSV). And Paul's conviction about divine aid is equally sure: "No temptation has overtaken you that is not common to man. God is faithful, and he will not let you be tempted beyond your strength, but with the temptation will also provide the way of escape that you may be able to endure it" (1 Corinthians 10:13 RSV). Hebrews' anonymous penman is even more specific: "For in that he himself hath suffered being tempted, he is able to succour them that are tempted" (Hebrews 2:18). It should be pointed out here that there is no contradiction between James and the writer of Hebrews. God, whose fundamental nature is Spirit, cannot be tempted to evil. God incarnate in human flesh in Jesus Christ has subjected Himself to being tempted so as to share our human infirmities. Unless God's Son could identify with fallen man in every way except in our yielding to sin, He could not have become our Savior.

Our Temptations Are Christ's

One of the loftiest concepts of the Church is amplified in the twelfth chapter of the first epistle to the church at Corinth. This concept grew out of Saul's conversion on the Damascus Road. En route to Damascus to persecute the Christians, the young rabbi was apprehended by the living Lord who asked, "Saul, Saul, why do you persecute me?" (Acts 9:4). Not until then did the soon-to-be apostle to the Gentiles realize that persecuting the Church is the same as persecuting the Lord Himself. Later, probably in the deserts of Arabia, he came to realize that the Church is "the body of Christ." He even added, when writing to the Church at Corinth, that we are each "individually members of it" (1 Corinthians 12:27).

Clearly this suggests that when Satan attacks either the Church or any true believer within it, he is attacking Christ. It could not be otherwise if we are the members of His body. Thus, we are not only tempted *in Christ*, as we earlier affirmed, but Christ is also tempted in us! Now we know that Jesus has already conquered temptation, therefore, the Christian has only to trust the victory of the Lord in order to find victory for himself. As long as man and Christ share the onslaughts of life the conquest is sure. Only the person who sets out to prove his own strength by resisting temptation is destined to defeat. We must "put on the whole armor of God, that [we] may be able to stand against the wiles of the devil. For we are not contending against flesh and blood, but against the principalities, against the powers, against the world rulers of this present darkness, against the spiritual hosts of wickedness in the heavenly places" (Ephesians 6:11-12 RSV). Here the biblical injunction of the apostle is in order: "Let anyone who thinks that he stands take heed lest he fall" (1 Corinthians 10:12 NEB).

As the believer is already judged in Christ's death, so he is already conqueror in Christ's temptation. By this is not meant that personal temptation is not real. On the contrary, it is real. But it is a share in the suffering of our Lord and, as a result, is a share in the conquest also. As we understand this to be so, we begin to see the intent of the otherwise strange petition in the model prayer of our Lord: "Do not bring us to the test, but save us from the Evil One" (Matthew 6:13 RSV). Christ grants this request Himself. No longer are we led into temptation as were those who lived before the advent of Jesus. They had slim chance, but we have the certainty of victory because the temptations have already come to Jesus and been conquered on our behalf. He is tempted *in* us and we find the power to conquer *in* Him. Either we win in Him or we lose by ourselves.

The Values That Come to Us

James, the brother of our Lord, had hardly completed his epistolary greeting until he began to urge the Jewish Christians, "Count it all joy, my brethren, when you meet various trials, for you know that the testing of your faith produces steadfastness" (James 1:2 RSV). What could be more desirable for the child of God than to become unwavering in his faithfulness, capable of standing tall and straight in the midst of all the raging storms that buffet him in the world? James had found that one learns to stand up, to take it on the chin as he is exposed to the severest testings. Peter would have agreed wholly: "After you have suffered a little while, the God of all grace, who has called you to his eternal glory in Christ, will himself restore, establish, and strengthen you" (1 Peter 5:10-11 RSV). Restoration and establishment—those are mighty words to describe the end of temptation. William James, the American philosopher, once said, "No one has ever really graduated in the school of life until he has been well tempted".

Not to be overlooked is the comforting word with which the temptation of Jesus is concluded: "Then the devil left him, and behold, angels came and ministered to him" (Matthew 4:11 RSV). One value of temptation is the joyous peace that follows in its wake. To have been conscious of the sustaining presence of God in the midst of the fray, is reward enough in itself. But to have added to that the ministry of the holy angels as an aftermath is a glorious thing indeed.

All of us have felt the calm after the storm and how refreshing it is. What we often fail to recognize, however, is that if there had been no storm no one would have noticed the calm. Furthermore, unfortunately the Christian sometimes basks in the warmth of divine victory, without pausing to thank God for His power in which we conquer, and His comforting follow up that heals open wounds.

One other value should be mentioned. It is Peter again who points out, "Be sober, be watchful. Your adversary the devil prowls around like a roaring lion, seeking someone to devour. Resist him, firm in your faith, knowing that the same experience of suffering is required of your brotherhood throughout the world" (1 Peter 5:8-9 RSV). Here we see that temptation is a communal affair. It is something the Church does together. And community brings a feeling of solidarity and strength. We do not suffer alone. Rather we face the Tempter in community, in a community whose Head is Christ Himself.

Relation of Temptation To the World to Come

Were nothing beyond this human experiment anticipated as a reward for loyalty in the acid tests of temptation, the whole thing would be a cruel joke played on humanity by an unfeeling and impersonal Fate or sadistic deity. All the hardships, suffering, and pain so generously displayed about us must be seen in the perspective of preparation for another life. Otherwise no meaning can be found at all for the enigmatic existence of human kind. No other philosophy of life is open to us except these two extremes. It is the presupposition that this life is a training ground for another which underlies the writing of this book.

From the non-canonical *Agrapha* (sayings of Jesus purported to be true by early writers not included in the Bible) come the words, "No man can obtain the kingdom of heaven that hath not passed through temptation." To be sure, the Kingdom of heaven is a present reality, which one enters now by faith in the atoning work of Him who brought that kingdom near. Nevertheless, the full reward awaits the perfecting of the kingdom in the return of Christ and the millennial reign (Matthew 19:28). Even then there will be more for the faithful as, following the 1,000 years of Messianic peace, "a new heaven and a new earth" appear (Revelation 21:1). This is the living hope and the "inheritance which is imperishable, undefiled, and unfading, kept in heaven for you, who by God's power are guarded through faith for a salvation ready to be revealed in the last time" (1 Peter 1:3-5 RSV).

The transitory and preparatory nature of temptation is beautifully revealed in the descriptive verses that follow the passage quoted above. Encouraging for the elect in the Lord is the promise: "In this you rejoice [the hope and inheritance just mentioned], though now for a little while you may have to suffer various trials [temptations], so that the authenticity of your faith, more precious than gold which though perishable is tested by fire, may redound to praise and glory and honor at the revelation of Jesus Christ" (1 Peter 1:6-7 RSV). According to the Petrine understanding of temptation, we are to be happy because it is necessary, temporary, and has something to do with getting us ready for the coming of the Lord.

Jesus had said essentially the same thing much earlier to the disciples. The Twelve had gotten into a dispute about preeminence, and the Master reminded them that the significant thing is not man's position here but his reward in the coming age. Obviously, the Lord was not afraid of being branded other worldly. Hear His promise: "You are those who have continued with me in my trials [temptations]; as my Father appointed a kingdom for me, so do I appoint for you that you may eat and drink at my table in my kingdom, and sit on thrones judging the twelve tribes of Israel" (Luke 22:28-30 RSV). Can there be any doubt as to where Simon Peter learned about the value of temptation in relation to the world to come? He learned it directly from the Lord

Being the brother of Jesus, James would naturally have some personal insight even though he did not become a believer until after the resurrection. It is absolutely amazing how completely this formerly envious brother came later to identify with the teaching of Mary's elder son. What he says about the role of temptation sounds enough like the Master that he may have been quoting Him verbatim: "Blessed is the man who endures trial [temptation], for when he has stood the test he will receive the crown of life, which God has promised to those who love him" (James 1:12 RSV). The word for *blessed* in the original Greek of the New Testament is *makarios* and is the same as that used by Jesus at the beginning of each beatitude. A better rendering might be "to be congratulated." James is actually suggesting that one deserves congratulations if he is tempted, because each trial provides a means of sharing both the suffering of Christ and the crown to be worn by the faithful Bride in the world to come.

It may seem unfair to some that seduction to be involved in bad things should be allowed for people who are trying to avoid evil. What must be remembered is that temptation is a natural part of the world, as natural as dirt, smog, and irritating fumes. God could have simply permitted such things to do us in with no recourse to combat them. But in grace and love, He has so created man and his world that temptation to evil can be overcome and good can come from it, the final outcome being better than if such seductive influences had not been allowed.

O Jesus, I have promised to serve Thee to the end;
Be Thou forever near me, my Master and my Friend:
I shall not fear the battle if Thou art by my side,
Nor wander from the pathway if Thou wilt be my guide.

O let me feel Thee near me! The world is ever near;
I see the sights that dazzle, the tempting sounds I hear;
My foes are ever near me, around me and within;
But, Jesus, draw Thou nearer, and shield my soul from sin.

O let me hear Thee speaking, in accents clear and still,
Above the storms of passion, the murmurs of self-will;
O speak to reassure me, to hasten or control;
O speak, and make me listen, Thou guardian of my soul.

O Jesus, Thou hast promised to all who follow Thee
That where Thou art in glory, there shall Thy servant be;
And, Jesus, I have promised to serve Thee to the end;
O give me grace to follow, my Master and my Friend.

—John E. Bode, 1816—1874

— Chapter 7 —

Persecution as a Part
of the Plan

How Persecution Differs from Temptation

Temptation arises from two general sources: Satan and the imperfect desires of the heart. The Bible says of the latter source, "Each man is tempted when he is drawn away by his own sin; and sin, when it is full grown, bringeth forth death" (James 1:14-15). Thus, we perceive that temptation is objective only in its Satanic attacks from without; it is subjective in the human proneness that has its seat in the heart. Though people may be used as instruments of the devil to effect temptation, the source of the problem is not to be traced to other persons. Temptation may be said to lie within the realm of the spirit—both demonic and human.

Persecution is different. Its source is purely objective and comes about as a direct attack upon man by other men. If men are employed in some way to carry out the devil's plan through temptation, it is almost always true that the human instrument has no malicious intent. In persecution, however, the premeditated objective is to hurt, to tear down, and to destroy another person. No one persecutes another with the belief that such a relationship will enhance their mutual enjoyment. In the scriptures, the persecutor is always cast in a vicious light. He is depicted as one bent on hurting others, often for the sheer kick that he gets out of it. Persecution, then, arises out of the unregenerate heart as a natural opposition to the regenerate nature of others. And Satan never misses the opportunity to take advantage of this Adamic animosity.

While temptation, if succumbed to, may bring a measure of pleasure immediately, persecution creates suffering of the most stringent kind at once. The latter often appears to be more devastating because its hurt is so much more readily seen. In reality, of course, it is the reward or lack of it in the world to come which really counts. No one can say whether temptation or persecution is the worse method of molesting the believer. We might note, nonetheless, that there is a degree of temptation somewhere in all persecution, though there may be no persecution at all in temptation. Although there are exceptions to every rule, persecution usually arises from human animosity while temptation has its origin in an animus that is thoroughly demonic.

A Way of Life

No one enjoys being persecuted unless he is suffering from a case of paranoia that enables him to commiserate himself in unpleasantness. Such people have a clearly defined emotional or mental defect. Normally, human beings flee from the first sign of such harsh treatment by their fellows. To run away, regardless as to how rational the decision may look, is as foreign to the life of discipleship as is the masochistic desire to go searching for the chance to be hurt. We do not have to hunt out troublesome experiences, nor is there the

116

slightest reason to think that they can be avoided. They are a part of life, a necessary part. Christ referred to the persecution of "the prophets who were before you" (Matthew 5:12). There is nothing new about it. Socrates and Seneca are examples of men who were persecuted and finally put to death by a society that disagreed with their philosophies. This sort of thing happens not only to Christians but often to anyone with whom someone else is vehemently in opposition. Even the psalmists, the singers in Israel, complain in constant refrain that their days were crammed with hardships brought on by men with evil intentions.

Having been through some of the bitterest sieges of persecution imaginable, the apostle Paul is confident that every believer must be prepared for a similar fate. So that Timothy may not be caught by surprise, Paul says to him, "Indeed, all who desire to live a godly life in Christ Jesus will be persecuted, while evil men and imposters will go on from bad to worse, deceivers and deceived" (2 Timothy 3:12-13). In fact, the persecution that came to the prophets who stood for truth and righteousness has waxed worse and worse across the centuries. Somewhere in the world at this moment the severity of man's wrath against truth is being bravely felt by devout and holy souls. This way of life known to the godly must become more and more unbearable until it reaches its zenith in the terrible seven years of tribulation at the end of the age (Revelation 13:1-10). Already we are witnessing yellow flags on the horizon warning of the impending onslaught against Christianity.

The form of persecution is not always the same. In the first three centuries of the Christian enterprise, thousands of believers were burned at the stake or fed to the hungry beasts. Those were bloody times, and human flesh was cheap. According to Jesus there will be a repeat performance of those days as we approach the end of earthly history. In isolated areas, since the time of Constantine to the present, man has been subjected to similar kinds of suffering. In the civilized world of the West, it is insisted that there is freedom from such ghastly treatment. Even where this is so, there is still persecution of the Christian. Persecution can take the form of social rejection, unkind criticism, and harmful jokes about another's faith, which wound as deeply as lion's teeth. Some dedicated disciples of Christ are daily in the fires of humiliating treatment handed out by persons who ought to know better.

"Do not be surprised at the fiery ordeal which comes upon you to prove you," writes the chief of the disciples, "as though something strange were happening to you. But rejoice in so far as you share Christ's sufferings, that you may also rejoice and be glad when his glory is revealed. If you are reproached for the name of Christ, you are blessed, because the spirit of glory and of God rests upon you, therefore, let those who suffer according to God's will do right and entrust their souls to a faithful Creator" (1 Peter 4:12-19 RSV). And what he says about the physical suffering of his time may just as aptly be said of the social and mental anguish of modern persecution in the civilized countries of the world.

Why People of Faith Are Mistreated

Most persecution comes about because of dislike for an individual. Often it is not actually known to the abuser why he dislikes the person whom he cannot resist attacking. He does not try to make life difficult for everybody whom he does not like, just some of them. And the reason for the selection is either ignored or excused. When a reason is voiced it is seldom an honest one.

Religious leaders and political rulers of Jesus' day disliked the carpenter from Nazareth with an unholy hatred. His days were haunted by the crafty designs to ensnare Him in His teaching. On numerous occasions, they would have harmed the Lord bodily if so many of the common people of the land had not deterred them. Finally, the angry clerics coerced the suspicious Romans into letting the hated carpenter be crucified. Charges were not in agreement and evidence was nowhere to be found for any of them, yet by bribery and intimidation the hostile religious leaders got their way and our Savior was nailed to a cross.

They accused Him of breaking their laws, of desecrating the Sabbath, of tampering with tradition. They insisted that He was subversive, some kind of self-appointed king who desired to overthrow the Roman empire. They even accused Jesus of blasphemy in claiming to be equal with God. But they never got around to being honest enough to tell the truth. Their hatred for Christ was not due to any of their trumped-up charges. No, they disliked Him because He made them feel guilty!

Men do not like to live in the presence of holiness. In such company our soil cannot be hidden. Our self-righteousness does a pretty good job fooling folk until it is exposed in the presence of the real thing. To live in the same city with Jesus Christ was a sobering, revealing, damning experience. Either the religious leaders had to admit their sham and acknowledge the Lordship of Christ or they had to get rid of Him! They chose to hide their guilt by disposing of the Light.

It is the same old story. Real Christians are "the light of the world" (Matthew 5:14) who continue the mission of Him who is "the true light that enlightens every man" (John 1:9). "And this is the judgment, that the light has come into the world, and men loved darkness rather than light, because their deeds were evil. For everyone who does evil, hates the light" (John 3:19-20). Christians are disliked because they throw needed light on the unregenerate nature of the world. It is much easier to try to put out the light or render it less illuminating by caustic persecution than it is to correct what the light exposes as being false in one's life. Persecution arises out of a feeling of guilt in the heart of the persecutor.

Did not the Lord warn the Twelve that they would "be hated by all for my name's sake"? (Matthew 10:22, Mark 13:13, Luke 21:17). What makes us believe today that the Christian way is ever going to become the desired way for all peoples? Nothing is clearer than Jesus' strong warning as remembered by John: "If the world hates you, you know that it has hated me before it hated you. If you were of the world, the world would love its own; but because you are not of the world, but I chose you out of the world, therefore, the world hates you . . . If they persecuted me, they will persecute you . . . If I had not done among them the works which no one else did, they would not have sin; but now they have seen and hated both me and my Father" (John 15:18-24 RSV, see also 17:14). If language has any meaning at all, guilt in the presence of righteousness is here stated to be the cause for persecution.

A Boon for the Church

Remove persecution from the Christian Church and it will die. There is something about suffering for righteousness that makes the Church strong. Not only did the early

Church of the first three centuries thrive because it was still fresh and alive, but it was fresh and alive because it was engaged in a life work that brought fierce resistance. Great struggle was needed to stay alive, and the harder the struggle, the sturdier grew the Church. It is often remarked that the blood of the martyrs was the seed of the Church. As difficult as it must have been for the pagan world to comprehend, every martyred saint seemed to give birth to a dozen more. The whole book of Acts tells how every new wave of persecution advanced the Christian cause, and the story is among the most exciting ever written.

Jonathan Swift once wrote, "I never saw, heard, nor read, that the clergy were beloved in any nation where Christianity was the religion of the country. Nothing can render them popular but some degree of persecution". Certainly the Christian minister is not interested in being popular, but it is a fact that the clergy have been most influential in helping shape philosophy where they were most savagely treated. And what is true of the clergy is also true of the laity. Swift's observation should have been more inclusive, since there was no reason to use the word *clergy* instead of the term *Christians*. The modern institutional church of the West has received very little if any persecution in the past. When earlier in these pages it was observed that persecution of Christians is always taking place somewhere in the world, we were referring to individual followers of Jesus rather than the church as a whole. None but the spiritually blind and the intellectually ignorant could fail to discern the reason for this. Our contemporary religious organizations have become so much like the unregenerate world in which they exist that the presence of the church no longer makes anyone feel guilt. For this reason, there is a growing movement across the land by local church groups who are withdrawing from traditional institutions and establishing their own independent congregations. The world never hates the church in its non-prophetic role. Only when the church does what it is supposed to do does it find itself in trouble from the secular world. Without question the institution of the church, where apostasy has become entrenched, is disliked and sometimes despised because it is so sterile and irrelevant. But when it does not stand as a condemnation of the world's sin, it is not persecuted. No one sees it as being worth the effort to attack. The church is just ignored.

To ignore the early Church was out of the question. Challenging the pagan culture was an organized body of Christians who refused to compromise with the latest fads in theology, rejected the immoral philosophy of their time, and gladly died before they would complement a world hostile to the truth as revealed in Jesus Christ. Sometimes overlooked is the fact that the early Church did not spend its time demonstrating in the streets against something they disagreed with, nor did they bombard Caesar's palace with a demand that laws be changed so as to force everyone to be like themselves. They had a much higher purpose. They never expected unregenerate people to act like Christians. It was obvious that they could not do any such thing. They just told the wonderful story of Jesus and His love and offered everyone they met an opportunity to discover what life is all about. If they had just shut up, refrained from witnessing, and joined in the life style of their worldly minded neighbors there would have been no problem. No one would have persecuted the Church. They could have held their services of worship and kept up a respectable appearance and everyone would have overlooked it. The only trouble was that, if such a thing had happened, the Christian Church would have died.

What the contemporary church needs today is resistance—not from its more dedicated members who deplore the nauseating spirit of tolerant syncretism, but resistance from a pagan culture that has become angry because its sin has been exposed and condemned. When the Christian Church lives up to its true mission and learns to live in close communion with its Lord, the whole institution suffers persecution instead of tolerance.

The Galatians are cautioned about those who do not want to be "persecuted for the cross of Christ" (Galatians 6:12). Is it not significant that the absence of persecution in our time is due to neglect of preaching and witnessing about the cross that characterized the community of faith in an earlier day? Wherever and whenever the cross is exalted as the extreme to which man's sin has brought him and the length to which God's love has gone, it becomes impossible to avoid persecution. In the same letter referred to above, Paul calls attention to this "stumbling block of the cross" (Galatians 5:ll).

Personal Worth of Persecution

Perhaps we may compare persecution to the hammer that strikes the anvil again and again as the hot steel is shaped into something useful. If the hammer represents the repeated persecution coming from the world, then the anvil symbolizes one's life and the shaped steel is that which the blow and corresponding resistance produce as a product of having lived. A world where everything runs completely free of friction would be intolerable, because man himself is made to live in the midst of tension. Not until the return of Christ in the Kingdom which is yet to be will we begin to enjoy the benefits of life without the debilitating tensions that squeeze the life out of us here. And then it will happen solely because the Prince of Peace will reign and "we shall be like Him" (1 John 3:2).

As long as we live in this world men will need opposition. We are learning that opposition is the womb of creativity. Little would ever be achieved without it. The story is told about a pastor making a call at a nursing home where he stopped to speak to a very old lady and inquire after her health. "Thank you, sir," replied the old lady. "Yes, indeed, I've got a great deal to be thankful for. I've got two teeth left and they're opposite each other." Not even teeth are of much value unless they are in a position to resist one another.

The Roman church had it in writing that tribulation "produces endurance, and endurance produces character, and character produces hope, and hope does not disappoint us" (Romans 5:3-5 RSV). Withstanding the avalanche of persecution heaped upon the loyal disciple of Christ is far from easy, but it is most rewarding. Each time one is battered by hostile attacks without yielding to pressure to compromise with the foe, he builds up additional resistance which may be needed as the conflict escalates. It is almost like having an inoculation of flu germs to build up one's body against a possible epidemic. What an old song said of temptation may appropriately be said of persecution: "Each victory will help you some other to win".

Failure to point out that there are eternal rewards would be to tell only half of the story. In concluding the Beatitudes, our Lord said, "Blessed are they who are persecuted for righteousness' sake, for theirs is the kingdom of heaven" (Matthew 5:10). In the next verse, He elaborates and specifically indicates a future state of blessedness: "Your reward is great in heaven." In John's vision of the heavenly realm, he sees a great multitude clothed in white and singing praises unto the Lamb. And he is told that "these are they who have come out of the great tribulation; they have washed their robes and made them white in the blood of the Lamb" (Revelation 7:14 RSV). Paul and Barnabas, on their missionary tour to strengthen the young churches that had been planted in Asia, exhorted the Christians "to continue in the faith . . . saying that through many tribulations we must enter the kingdom of God" (Acts 14:22).

God will not look for diplomas when we stand before Him at last, but for scars. How ashamed we will be to appear in the presence of Him whose hands and feet were wounded for us unless we also "bear on [our] body the marks of Jesus" (Galatians 6:17 RSV). This in no way is a cry for the stigmata which Francis of Assisi bore upon his hands, but a plea for a willingness to "endure hardness as a good soldier of Jesus Christ" (2 Timothy 2:3).

An old story is told of two little children who were climbing up the steep side of a rather rugged hill near their home. Naturally the little boy was considerably ahead of his playmate if for no other reason than to prove his prowess and superiority. The small girl was complaining about all the rocks which jutted out of the ground and slowed her down. "Come on," cried the boy, "the bumps are what you climb on!" And so it is true that persecutions may either slow us down or become stepping stones into the kingdom. It all depends on how we react.

Paranoia Is Not a Christian Virtue

Inevitably, some within the Christian community will give the impression of being depressed all the time. To hear them tell it, their lot is harder than anyone else's. Nobody has as much trouble as they. Among the many exemplary qualities seen in the early disciples is the inescapable presence of radiance. Persecutions, tribulations, beatings, confiscation of property, banishment, even death—none of these things ever got them down. Never do we sense that any of them ever felt sorry for himself. Christ had come that their "joy might be full" (1 John 1:4) and thus they rejoiced with "joy unspeakable and full of glory" (1 Peter 1:8). In fact, joy is the dominant note of the New Testament Church. Not until the glow was allowed to wear off did some within the fellowship begin to be depressed and miserable.

Quite frankly, it needs to be affirmed that a miserable Christian is a contradiction. Of course, the followers of the Lord will have their moments of distress and grief. We all have moods as long as we live. But miserable? Never! The world is miserable, let the Christian be happy, hilariously happy. And if one is a real Christian, he is. Deep inside him there is peace and joy unruffled by what may happen in the world. His days will be filled with concern and he will be disturbed by what he sees happening in a world ruled by Satan. Jesus shared this concern with us. But if a man is miserable inside, he has never found the life of Christ.

Because this is true, paranoia must be branded once and for all time as an unchristian attitude. A paranoid is one who cannot understand why everybody is down on him, especially since he is such a grand person. In both assumptions, such a person is outside the way of Christ. First, there is no known reason why any Christian should think everybody is down on him. Nor is there any reason for wondering why persecutions do come from somebody. Jesus left no confusion about that. Second, no true Christian can harbor inflated opinions of himself as though he deserves better treatment than that which was given to Jesus. "The disciple is not above his master, nor the servant above his lord. It is enough for the disciple that he be as his master, and the servant as his lord. If they have called the master of the house Beelzebub, how much more shall they call them of his household?" (Matthew 10:24-25). To think of ourselves as being entitled to freedom from persecution is completely unacceptable.

The Dangers of a Martyr Complex

Stories have come down to us from the ancient Church about men and women who literally tried to get themselves killed for the glory of Christ. As the years passed the Church emphatically categorized levels of Christian attainment, that of martyrdom being the highest of all. He who gave his life was assured a place in heaven as well as in the history of the Church. Under such ecclesiastical influence and holy sanction there were those who made martyrdom the objective of their days. If by some strange and unexplainable twist they were never burned or thrown alive to the lions, the rest of their days were spent in the certainty of having somehow failed God. For them, to miss the crown of martyrdom was the worst fate of all.

While we are to glory in tribulation and rejoice in persecution, great care must be taken lest we confuse the means with the end. Hardness for the believer can be of inestimable value in preparing us for life here and in the next world. To seek after it, however, is not encouraged or condoned by Scripture. Even Jesus prayed for release from His own crucifixion if such a change in plans could be in line with the Father's will (Matthew 26:39). Christ loved life and was loathe to die at thirty-three. His was no martyr complex, and those who attempt to force Him into that mold do a terrible injustice to the biblical image of the historical Jesus.

To run intentionally into the life of martyrdom is related to the act of suicide. And to force persecution unnaturally is as presumptuous as it would have been for Jesus to throw Himself from the temple tower. No one has the right to throw away this life just because there is another one promised. There are no shortcuts to heaven. Let us never think that there is something Christlike about detouring around the responsibilities of living in this world until He is ready to call us. Patience is as much a part of pleasing the Lord as is tribulation or even martyrdom.

How to Handle Persecution

Exposure to the rigors of persecution produces various reactions. Some literally collapse without even making an effort to stand up to the onslaughts. Not unusual is it for one to struggle for a while and then surrender to the less demanding life of compromise. Needless to say, this kind of person fights in his own strength and has not learned to depend on the indwelling Christ. Of course, if one's Christianity is only a nominal thing, there is no experience of a personal Lord to which he can fly his flag. With people like this, the Word of God has been heard and a superficial and emotional response has been made. Their response is so shallow that "they believe for a while and in time of temptation [or persecution] fall away" (Luke 8:13).

Unfortunately there are those who grow querulous and complaintive toward God. The Lord is doubted, His love is suspected, and the divine design is missed entirely. Others, while not blaming the Lord, become vicious in the treatment of their persecutors. Like an irritable dog, they snap back and even bite. Vengeance is not left to the Judge of all the earth, but it becomes the prerogative of the molested believer. In spite of the fact that we live in a dispensation of grace, such persons revert at times to that of the law where the philosophy by which men lived was "eye for eye, tooth for tooth, hand for hand, foot for foot, burn for burn, wound for wound, stripe for stripe" (Exodus 21:24-25). Though there may be no actual physical abuse as in the Old Testament, words and attitudes can be just as vicious and damaging to the value of persecution and to one's witness.

Christ introduces us to a totally new concept of life in the discourse known as the Sermon on the Mount. Commenting on the law mentioned above, the Lord requires that we turn the other cheek, give our cloak as well as our coat when demanded, and offer to go two miles when conscripted to go one. He even goes so far as to say, "Love your enemies and pray for those who persecute you" (Matthew 5:5:39-44). When writing to the Romans, the apostle to the Gentiles emphatically states, "Bless those who persecute you; bless and do not curse them . . . Never avenge yourselves, but leave it to the wrath of God; for it is written, Vengeance is mine, I will repay, says the Lord" (Romans 12:14-19 RSV). Then he quotes from the Old Testament a proverb about being kind to one's enemies. In doing so "you will heap coals of fire on his head" (Proverbs 25:22). Paul is not suggesting that our kindness should be given with the intent of building such a fire. That would be an unchristian motivation of the worst type. What He is doing is nothing other than making an observation that this is always what happens.

Dr. Stuart Holding used to tell a story about a private in his company who was a deeply committed Christian. One evening he returned to the barracks tired, wet, and muddy. But, before he tumbled into his bed, he knelt down to pray. Reaching for his own wet, sloppy boots, Holding threw them at the soldier. The boy never moved from his position of prayer. The following morning Stuart Holding found his boots beautifully polished and placed by his own bed. That was the Christian's reply to persecution, and it broke the heart of the persecutor. That day Dr. Holding accepted Christ as his Savior.

He who discovers and accepts gladly the truth that we are fools for Christ's sake will begin to see the glorious unfolding of the divine plan, a design of eternal dimension which no one sees who continues to revel in his self sufficiency. To some, it will look as though the apostle extraordinarius has gone to unnecessary lengths when he pens these words: "When reviled, we bless; when persecuted, we endure; when slandered, we try to conciliate; we have become, and are now, as the refuse of the world, the offscouring of all things unto this day" (1 Corinthians 4:12-13 RSV). But he had learned with Peter that "the Lord knows how to rescue the godly from trial" (2 Peter 2:9 RSV) and that the experience of joy that is better than all our human means of defending ourselves. And it is well worth waiting for until the Lord is ready to give that deliverance.

— Chapter 8 —

The Presence of Pain

A World Full of Hurt

Everywhere one looks there is suffering and anguish. Multiplied thousands are victims of war, poverty, disease, man's inhumanity to man, and freakish disasters intended by no one at all. As terrible as war is in its destruction of human life, more people are killed or maimed in automobile accidents than in any and all wars. Hospitals are overcrowded with patients whose bodies are mangled and broken in the day to day struggle to make a living. Doctors' offices are crowded to capacity, and even persons with appointments often wait all day for examination and treatment. In the larger metropolitan areas, the piercing screams of police cars and ambulances are heard almost constantly. Even in the small towns hardly a day passes without such sounds to remind us of suffering and death.

Among the ever-present sites that keep us sobered to the reality of pain and the prevalence of anguish are the expanding complexes known as nursing or convalescent homes. Most of these institutions for the infirm and aging are

cheerful enough and staffed with compassionate person-
nel, but they still spell sadness for their many residents
and create feelings of guilt for families who are forced to
deposit their senior members there. At a time when people
ought to be enjoying peace and quiet after a lifetime of hard
work, the corridors are punctuated with the distressing cries
of physical pain and mental distress.

In spite of the great strides in medical science and the
many scourges that have been conquered, it seems that there
is more misery today than ever before. Part of this impression is due to the growing population, public treatment of
many diseases which were formerly cared for at home, and
the easy availability of hospitalization insurance or federal
medical aid. But that is not the whole picture. Dread diseases attack more and more people every year. Much suffering seems so senseless and useless.

With all the abundance enjoyed by some more highly
developed nations, other countries suffer the pangs of hunger and a lack of medical technicians and supplies. Great
numbers of children die from starvation and related illnesses
every day while multitudes of us suffer from overweight.
And the worst part of it is that there seems to be no way by
which the average citizen can do much about what is happening beyond his own community. He is made to feel guilty,
but the world government of which he is a part has become
so complex that his concern has few practical outlets. Thus,
suffering continues to increase faster than our scientific and
technological remedies can handle.

War takes its toll of the world's finest young men each
year. No sooner than one hot spot is cooled and troops
brought out than another erupts to scorch and burn the
land and the people. Torture, rape, and murder are not

confined to the battlefields of war. Personal assaults with intent to harm or kill increase annually on the civilized streets of our cities, on college campuses, and just about everywhere men have to live together.

Added to the physical hurt of our planet is the mental suffering that has called into existence a whole specialized field of psychiatry with growing numbers of clinics to care for the mentally disturbed and emotionally distressed among us. A new and rapidly expanding branch of this service is devoted to treatment of drug addiction, especially among the young. Hardly a family can be found in these times where either some youthful member has not experimented with drugs or some older member has not leaned on tranquilizers or anti-depressants. Already the seeds of suffering have been planted which may produce agonizing fruits in years to come.

Sometime ago a cartoon appeared in one of our syndicated newspapers, which portrayed the world globe with a thermometer in its mount, an ice cap on its head, and a bandage around its middle. A physician was taking its pulse and, shaking his head sadly, was saying, "You are very sick. You are allergic to yourself!" That may have been a penetrating and honest look at our times. The diagnosis was probably correct. We have about decided that suffering is a part of living with ourselves. As long as we are human and the world remains the world there will be suffering and hurt.

Why Must There Be Suffering?

No question has challenged the philosophers or baffled the common man more than the why of suffering. For as long as humankind has been capable of thought the air has been rife with this puzzling complaint, sometimes bitter reflection. The question is heard in the midst of death, illness, depression, separation, hunger, and fear. Manifestly, the degree of intensity with which the question is asked has a double hinge —the seriousness of suffering and the innate temperament of the sufferer. It takes far less hurt to touch the raw nerve of some than of others. But everyone has a nerve somewhere, and when the probe digs deeply enough, he cries in pain and petulance.

A little girl had fallen and skinned her knees on the pavement. After her mother brushed off the dirt, applied a healing cream, and dried her face, the small girl was heard to say almost wistfully, "Wouldn't it be wonderful if the whole world was cushioned?" Indeed, it would. Or so we are inclined to think. Either one should have been created so as not to fall or the surface on which he falls ought to have been padded. Why the Creator did not take care of one or the other of these preferred possibilities is a source of considerable wonder.

Almost universally man believes that life on the earth would have been greatly improved if pain were not a part of it. What is usually not even recognized is that life did begin without suffering in the garden of Eden and, when it is finally reclaimed in the paradise of God, will return to that ideal state again. Not until after Adam and Eve had sinned was there any hint of pain. It was the result of sin which added pain to childbirth. And if there is pain in birth, then there is continual suffering since human life is always in the process of being born. The discomfort of making a living is the result of sin in human nature as is the reduced creativity of the soil itself. Plant life is affected by the appearance of thorns and briars. Animal life has also been subjected to a harder lot as illustrated in the curse upon one of its kind, the serpent. And all because of sin.

The human race must admit, therefore, that where there is sin there is bound to be suffering. It is also true that where there is holiness there is peace. But there are many extenuating circumstances that determine the balance, circumstances we know nothing about. Furthermore, the balance is never to be seen in any individual life. Life is lived in community and what equalization is possible in this world is to be witnessed only there. Did not Jesus have this community concept in mind, as well as that of the impartiality of the Father, when He said, "He makes his sun to rise on the evil and on the good, and sends rain on the just and on the unjust"? (Matthew 5:45 RSV). Only in the world to come will we see perfectly the balance that has been disguised during our stay on earth. And only in heaven will all pain be done away, both individually and in community, because only in heaven will sin be destroyed.

Personal Suffering and Personal Sin

It must be emphatically declared that acts of sin can and do produce suffering. One cannot sin without paying for it. Someone has to pay. The glory of the Christian gospel is that Christ has paid the penalty for our sin upon the cross. While this assures the believer that the final judgment on sin has already been faced and we are acquitted in our Redeemer, it does not necessarily let us off from the natural consequences of sin in this life. He who defies the laws of sanity and health must suffer for his foolishness. If he desecrates and defiles his body in alcohol, barbiturates, or sex, he cannot expect to be free from scourges that follow in the wake of such activity. Miracles do happen, but we usually have to face these earthly consequences. Becoming a Christian does not restore the use of a man's limbs that have been rendered useless by a fire into which he fell while drunk. "Whatever a man sows, that shall he also reap" (Galatians 6:7). It never fails.

A word of qualification is in order before going any further. What about those who throw caution to the winds, sow their wild oats, and die in their unbelief? Must we not acknowledge that some of them seem to evade such suffering altogether? To these questions there is only one answer, the answer found by the writer of Ecclesiastes: "Walk in the ways of your heart and the sight of your eyes. But know that for all these things God will bring you into judgment" (Ecclesiastes 11:9 rsv). That is, there is a day of reckoning for us all, a time when unforgiven sin must be met in punishment. Paul is saying apparently the same thing when he continues on the sowing-reaping theme: "For he who sows to his own flesh will from the flesh reap corruption; but he who sows to the Spirit will from the Spirit reap eternal life" (Galatians 6:8 rsv). Some suffering is reserved for the next world.

If it must be emphatically stated that sin does produce suffering, it must just as emphatically be pointed out that all suffering is not the direct result of personal sin. Job's friends were sure that he would not have been suffering as the account indicates unless he had sinned against the Lord. Of course, Job was just as sure that he had not been guilty of any such totally devastating sin. When the disciples asked Jesus who sinned that the man was born blind (John 9), himself or his parents, the answer was neither. There had been no parental or prenatal sin to cause the suffering of blindness. Christ found another reason entirely.

Much suffering is brought about solely because we are a part of the human race. We are a race of sinners and everything done by any one of us has some direct or indirect effect on all others. It is no exaggeration to say that a little boy in the African bush can stub his toe and the whole world cries "Ouch!" The solidarity of the human race is both a beautiful and a horrifying thing to contemplate. If it is true that "in Adam we all die" (1 Corinthians 15:22) so in Adam we all suffer and hurt together. Disease, poverty, war, and a million kinds of distress are all a part of the outworking of man's relatedness to every other man. Humanity is comprised of human beings. Every time any segment of that humanity acts in either a good or evil manner, the whole of humanity feels it.

To What End?

When the disciples asked the Lord why the man was born blind, Jesus sought to correct the perspective by explaining that they were asking the wrong question. A much better question would have been: to what end was he born blind? The tendency to blame God, or anyone else for that matter, disappears when we admit that there is an end involved in what happens to us. Fear, as well as bitterness, no longer stifles the man who sets himself to the task of discovering how and where good may come out of suffering. To react in complaintive resentment is to miss what value could be found in adverse circumstances of pain and anguish.

Illumination was available for the disciples as they confronted the enigma of human suffering. Nevertheless, when Jesus brought new light to bear on the question, they were hardly prepared for what He said. "Neither hath this man sinned, nor his parents, but that the works of God may be made manifest in him, I must work the works of him that sent me" (John 9:3-4). At first, this sounds as though God is a capricious deity who seeks self-glory in making men suffer so that He can heal them. Christ is saying nothing of the kind. What He is saying is that God can transform man's worst hurt into a thing of glory. The Lord had nothing to do with the origin of the man's blindness. A maze of biological and hereditary factors was involved in the blindness, factors so multitudinous and complex that medical scientists do not understand them even yet. Out of all this complicated misery, however, God can produce a glorious thing. And "the works of God" are not performed to solicit praise for God but to heal and redeem.

The scripture passage we have just quoted from John's Gospel is a perfect example how punctuation can alter the meaning of a statement. In the original texts of the Bible, there was no punctuation marks at all. These markings have been added in the translations. If we leave out the arbitrary comma placed at the end of verse 3, the words of our Lord take on an entirely different meaning: "Neither hath this man sinned, nor his parents. But that the works of God should be made manifest in him I must work the works of him that sent me." Jesus is warning His men not to get all tangled up in a theological problem. Instead, they should join Him in confronting the pressing question: "This is the way life is! Now what can we do to help this poor man through his ordeal?"

On another occasion, our Lord made a similar observation about the end of sickness and death. Mary and Martha had sent word to the Lord in Perea that Lazarus was sick at Bethany. Unlike His customary habit of going at once to relieve suffering, He remained where He was and sent a message that read, "This sickness is not unto death, but for the glory of God, that the Son of God might be glorified thereby" (John 11:4). Since it is so easy to miss the point, it must be pointed out that the word *glory* in the gospel of John invariably has to do with the crucifixion and resurrection of Christ. The one thing that brought glory to the Son, as well as to the Father, was the redemptive work of Jesus. If we read the incidents recorded in John's gospel which immediately follow the raising from the dead of Lazarus, it will be quickly noted that it was this miracle that finally precipitated the action of His enemies to get Him on the cross.

There is little reason to believe that the sisters either appreciated or understood what He meant until Lazarus had been raised from the dead. Even then the meaning of death had to be explained in light of eternity rather than just in respect to man's human parenthesis in time.

"The glory of God" is the salvation of man, his healing and final resurrection. The glorification of the Son is only another way of saying the same thing. When Christ is glorified it is man who profits since the glory of Jesus Christ lies in what He has done and is doing for us. God's day to day procedures are often unknown to us, but the end and final purpose should be clear. In the case of the blind man, it was healing and in that of Lazarus it was resurrection. In both cases the end result was a prelude to the world to come where health and life will be the possession of all.

A Divine Plan behind the Scene

The obvious is not always the whole story. Usually more is taking place out of sight to the natural eye and beyond the logic of the rational mind. At the time of the selling of young Joseph to the Midianites as a slave, there was no doubt that the future would be dark and full of suffering. Later the picture changed and the evil brothers, who had perpetrated the crime against Rachel's elder son, found themselves begging food at his feet in Egypt. Sensing their fear, Joseph, whose magnanimous spirit shames us all, said, "Fear not . . . you meant evil against me; but God meant it for good, to bring it about that many people should be kept alive, as they are today" (Genesis 50:19-20).

What seemed obvious to the envious brothers at the moment of their vicious action against Joseph was not the plan of God at all. And during those two years of imprisonment for a crime of which he was not guilty, it appeared that suffering had no meaning even to Joseph. The hour was to come, nevertheless, when God would allow Joseph to see what He was doing through the long, dark nights of his imprisonment.

In seventeenth-century England lived a profane young man whose praying wife led him to Christ in 1655. Literally consumed by his love for the God who had saved him from his past life, he began to preach. Five years later he was arrested for preaching without a license from the Established Church and thrown into Bedford jail where he remained for the next 12 years. No one had any idea what God was doing in all this suffering. But had John Bunyan not undergone that awful hardship, the world would be much poorer. It was while in that dismal cell that he wrote that famous allegory, *The Pilgrim's Progress*.

For nothing worse than preaching the gospel of Jesus Christ, the apostle John was banished to the island of Patmos. At least he had escaped the physical pain of martyrdom, which had been the lot of the other disciples. But the loneliness and mental torture of being exiled from his church and the people he loved was its own kind of suffering. Rome had meant the banishment to be an experience of unalleviated misery, but God had other plans for John. The lonely isle became a door to heavenly communion. There the apostle soared on wings of prophetic ecstasy, traversed the ages of time, and was permitted to glimpse the majestic events of the closing age. Unquestionably, the vision which has enriched the Church until this present hour would have been withheld from John and us if there had been no adversity to bring out the end time truth. In some way, his suffering made John sensitive to the realities of divine truth which could not have been received without what looked like an extremely harsh discipline.

Earlier in our study, we made reference to history's most classic illustration of suffering, the book of Job. An additional word is needed at this juncture. No one suffered more acutely than did Job. And many lessons can be profitably learned from a careful investigation of this ancient narrative. Among them is the observation that suffering is not always the result of sin. Where to draw the line is difficult to ascertain since Job, though "blameless and upright" (Job 1:2), was a sinner as all other men. But the point is that no specific sin produced the adversity he experienced. On the contrary, the severe treatment grew out of his unusual integrity.

Another lesson learned is that well-meaning friends can be wrong in their assumptions and can complicate one's problems unintentionally. Still another is that righteousness does not exempt anyone from the hurts of life on the earth. And yet another is that, while suffering is allowed by

God, it is not sponsored by Him. This one insight alone should give us help as we wrestle with the old enigma of pain in a world created and loved by God. A final lesson suggests that the righteous man is rewarded by the Lord if he retains his integrity rather than "curse God and die" (Job 2:10). Care must be taken not to misinterpret the earthly possessions, returned to and multiplied for Job, to imply that every situation must have the same kind of reward *now*. Some will have to wait even longer than Job, wait until "He will wipe away every tear from their eyes, and death shall be no more, neither shall there by mourning nor crying nor pain anymore, for the former things have passed away" (Revelation 21:4 RSV).

The Important thing to note is the careful way in which a loving God supervised all that Satan was allowed to do in carrying out his plan. There was a limit set for the adversary from the beginning. And in each new foray the Satanic intent and strategy of operation had to be checked out by a loving Father. What was obvious to the devil all along was that Job would weaken and blame God, that he would miss the purpose of suffering and lose its reward. God had other ends in view, which were completely opposite. Job himself, in the middle of chaos and personal confusion, began to sense the divine design when he replied to Eliphaz, "He knows the way that I take; when he has tried me, I shall come forth as gold" (Job 23:10).

It would be impossible anywhere to find a sufferer more undeserving of the hurts of living than was Jesus. Persons who reprimand God for not ending pain with the argument that He does not care or else has no power, are stopped cold at the cross of Calvary. If ever He would interfere with the lot of man as a member of the human race, it would surely be in the interest of His own Son. But He did not. And every anguish experienced by the redeeming Christ was felt also by the Father in heaven. God "spared not His own Son" (Romans 8:32) nor did He exempt Himself from suffering. It was in divine suffering that redemption came to the world. The world looked at the cross as irrevocable failure, but God's overriding plan was far different. Only on the far side of the cross was the end, toward which scourging and crucifixion were the means, clearly seen. Likewise, only on the far side in the world to come will the divine plan be fully revealed. All of us would do well to develop more patience, which is not resignation to blind fate but expectation of a loving disclosure.

Thorns Do Make Sweeter Music

As if persecution were not enough, Paul also endured some kind of gnawing, physical discomfort unrelated to the treatment rendered him by his enemies. Speculation has run wild about the nature of his problem. He calls it "a thorn in the flesh" (2 Corinthians 12:7). Whatever it was, Paul was harassed by it and sought its removal. Three times he asked the Lord to remove it. Each time the answer was, "My grace is sufficient for you, for my power is made perfect in weakness" (2 Corinthians 12:9). Far from being easy to accept, the apostle was ultimately forced to acknowledge that his ministry and Christian effectiveness were somehow enhanced by the acceptance of the thorn. In sharing the *thorn* of Christ, the disciple is made stronger than when he fails to understand the suffering of the Lord in the midst of his own self- sufficiency.

A story is told of a man who lived many years ago in a small town in England. His love of good music led him to collect great numbers of gramophone records. One evening he invited a fellow student of good music to listen to some of his recordings. In the course of the evening, he informed his friend that he was going to play a record twice and would like for him to listen carefully and then select the sound he liked better. At the end of the second playing, the friend chose the latter rendering because, as he said, "It was much purer and sweeter." When asked what made the difference, the host explained that the first time a needle was used and the second time the record was played with a thorn.

History's purest and sweetest people have been those whose music was produced by a thorn. Not all sufferers create music. Only those who accept it as a share in the disciplining and redeeming agony of humanity. Too many react so strenuously to the approach of pain that the whole experience is wasted in feeling sorry for themselves and wearing out everyone else with their sad details of undeserved misery. Once in a while, far too seldom, we meet a sensitive soul who suffers bravely, hardly ever mentions his hurts, fills the world where he lives with radiance, and makes everyone in his presence feel absolutely great. The song of joyful suffering is far more beautiful than is any song of pampered softness. Frankly, this latter type of singing is squeaky thin and quickly turns to boredom.

Years ago it was my good fortune to know a young woman whose days were filled with joy and beauty and whose radiant Christian witness seemed to pronounce a blessing upon everyone she met. When it was discovered that she had a rare form of inoperable cancer and that she had only a short time to live, she accepted her suffering with unimaginable grace. No one who knew her ever heard her complain, not one time. Toward the end of her stay in the hospital, shortly before she died, the woman who was staying by her bedside heard her say, "I think I know God now better than I ever did before." Magnificent! That is what suffering is designed to do.

If we could communicate with a dog being trained by its master, we would hear a very sad story. The dog does not like to be interfered with, to have its nature altered, its manners improved. To be washed and perfumed, trained to adopt the habits of the family, taught to eat without spilling its food, and monitored in its every move is enough to make any dog question its master's love. But later, after much discipline and *suffering*, the dog would begin to sense that it is loved more, better suited to living with man, and heir to a world never before possible for such a creature. Then, and only then, it would see how man, whose motives had been suspected, loved it through all the hurt. In fact, if the dog could reason, it would recognize that the hurt was actually a part of the love itself, at least integrally related to it. And the benefits received by the dog from the severity of the discipline would go beyond anything that either the dog or its master could have imagined.

The Element of Mystery

Explain it as we may, there remains much mystery in life and death. Try as we will, we cannot comprehend all the origins and destinies that are interwoven into the fabric of existence. Universities can tell us a great deal about a great many things, but their knowledge is of little help in the midst of terminal illness. Scientists and philosophers wax eloquent in their learned explanations until thrust into the midst of suffering and death. Then they are as speechless as anyone else. At this point man must resort to faith or he will despair in hopelessness. And when we enter the world of faith we are chin deep in mystery. No scientific method has been devised by which to prove anything in the world of faith. It is at this precise point in life that man falls back on God in childlike trust and confidence.

Looking at a tapestry being made by a friend, a man complained that he could see no pattern at all in what was undoubtedly supposed to have a design. How foolish he felt when told that he had been looking at the backside of the tapestry. Could it be that we, in our human finiteness, see only the backside of the divine design? Do only a few of the more saintly souls get a preview of what is to come? If we could see the plan of God full view, might not all of us feel exceedingly foolish in having questioned the Lord or impugned His motives in the midst of our hurt?

Suffering will be seen in different ways by different people. One's perspective is directly related to his concept of God. If God is aloof, disinterested, or helpless— suffering will have no meaning and will be cause for cursing and despair. If God is in this thing with us, concerned about us, and powerfully working out His good plan for us—suffering will not simply have a purpose but will be cause for joyous acceptance. From the center of this mystery, we can affirm that one does not have to know why if he knows Who.

— Chapter 9 —

Why Some Die So Young

Threescore and Ten Years

Almost refrain-like, the obituary column of the patriarchs report the average age of the ancients to have
been 800 to 900 years (Genesis 5). One of them, Enoch,
seems to be out of place because his earthly pilgrimage was
cut short at 365. But further reading indicates that he actually never died at all. Enoch was translated, caught away
unto heaven in an abrupt and premature exit from the world.

All sorts of explanations have been offered for the longevity of these ancient fathers of the human race. We are as
apt to be correct in taking the years to represent 12 months
each as we are in searching for some more rational clarification. More than likely, they just lived a long, long time.
Acceptance of that as factual does not aid us much in explaining why they lived so much longer than we. It is obvious to us all that hardly any of the patriarchs' modern
descendants live more than a tithe of their years.

For some reason, maybe nothing more than the attri-
tion of the human race as it accumulated the decay of sin,

147

by the time of the psalmist we are told: "The years of our life are threescore and ten, or even by reason of strength fourscore" (Psalm 90:10). Even with medical attempts at lengthening human life and the promise of increased longevity in the future, man still builds his plans around the figure of 70 years. While he hopes to live longer and acts at times like he is going to be here forever, he inwardly perceives that his days are confined, give or take a few years either way, to seven decades. In comparison to the patriarchs, contemporary men all die in infancy. Even at age 91, we would seem like young children.

Calendars are irrelevant to the nature of God. Time is divided naturally into seasonal periods, which, in ever recurring cycles, provide a rather exacting method of calculating time. The arrangement is for the benefit of man, however, not of God. Man has found the division of time into parts to be needful for designating events both past and present. Historical references would be impossible without such divisions. This includes months, days, and hours as well as years. So we have scientific, historical, and practical reasons for the calendar. But time is a continuum without interruption for the Creator. "Do not ignore this one fact . . . that with the Lord one day is as a thousand years, and a thousand years as one day" (2 Peter 3:8, see also Ps. 90:4). This means that, from God's vantage point, the number of years one lives is of no particular importance. His design for the world and everything in it is worked out on an eternal schedule that is not affected one way or the other by the age of man at his death. Earthly existence is only an interlude in the divine story of creation and redemption, and only a prelude to the life accessible to man by faith.

Regardless what may be true of the divine timelessness, man lives in the midst of time. We cannot opt for anything else. And the years advance faster than he is willing to admit. We keep trying to convince ourselves that we are still only boys and girls. Yet, we are finding gray hair in our combs lately. Our skin in wrinkling, and our breath is a little shorter than it used to be. Strange creaking in our back and legs appears out of nowhere. Whether we like it or not, the sundial is right—it is later than you think. The sand in the hourglass runs through more quickly than we can imagine and our 70 years are up before we have gotten started in the business of living. Threescore years and ten are not long, but if handled well, they are long enough. Let us never forget that the most important thing is not how long we live, but how well. Methuselah lived over 900 years. Jesus only 33. But what a difference!

An Allotment Cut Short

No matter how long man might live, he would never be satisfied. Even Methuselah at 969 may have felt that God ought to have given him more time. But humanity is handed a double grief when life's flame is snuffed out long before the expected day. To be sure, no certainty has accompanied the round number in Psalms. Nonetheless, every man convinces himself that something has gone wrong if his years are less than 70. It is almost as if we believe that we have the right to hold God to a promise He never made. And when our roughly *predestined* life span is cut short we immediately blame God for a breach of promise in permitting things to go awry.

Earthly life is a loan from the Lord. Man has nothing to do with starting his existence and nothing to do with ending it. Life belongs to God, not to us. Consequently, He has a right to do what He pleases with these bodies fashioned for our habitation. "You know not what shall be on the morrow. For what is your life? It is even a vapor that appeareth for a little time and then vanisheth away. For you ought to say, If the Lord will, we shall live, and do this, or that" (James 4:14-15). Shakespeare noted that life is "a walking shadow." And there was nothing original about his observation. The human race has known that since the beginning.

Still we are stunned and filled with questions when loved ones and friends leave us in the prime of their years. Unloading some parcels from the car one night, an automobile pulled up alongside me and, through the lowered window, a man's voice inquired as to the whereabouts of the pastor's home. Learning that the one with whom he spoke was the pastor, he parked quickly and came toward me talking all the while. He was saying, "We lost our little boy yesterday, and I would like for you to talk to my wife".

Once inside the parsonage, they unburdened their hearts. Their three-year-old son had just died from a heart condition that was much more serious than they had thought. They had no other children, and this boy was cherished deeply. The young parents were driving through the night from their home in Georgia to the grandparents' home and place of burial in Indianapolis, where the funeral was to be conducted the following day. The father's face was red. Apparently he had been crying. His wife was pale and quiet, her eyes showing deep hurt. Our paths had never crossed before, nor have they since. We were total strangers and yet, in their despair, they were asking me to tell the mother something that would help her through her grief. What does one say at a time like that?

Two British explorers came across a tomb in Egypt that had been sealed for more than 3,000 years. Inside was an exquisitely carved sarcophagus containing the remains of a little child. Over it were inscribed the words: "Oh my life, my love, my little one, would God I had died for thee." With tears running down their faces, the explorers backed out of the tomb with uncovered heads, sealed it back as it had been, without disturbing what was left of a very old sorrow. Not alone do the inscribed words betray the grief of ancient parents, but it also describes the stunned confusion faced by people in all generations who give up their loved ones while yet young.

Puzzling as the untimely deaths of children may be, we human beings are no less stunned when maturing adults are struck down before the sun has dropped much past high noon in their lives. Why mothers of little children are brought down to the grave at a time when no one in the world can fill their shoes is a matter of heartbreak for the entire neighborhood. Or why fathers who are depended on for food and shelter are taken away when families so desperately need their support is an enigma of the greatest magnitude. Why men and women, whose contribution to the world has such bright prospects, must die with all their music in them no one really knows. And to make matters even worse, why do some who are parasites on society seem to live forever? Why do persons who are quite wicked remain to spread their evil influence? As if the problem were not puzzling enough already, there is the additional question as to why the old and infirm are not permitted to die while the young and able are often refused life. Admittedly, we have no prepackaged answers, but there is some light that can help us through the darkness.

Deserving of Promotion

Did we really believe what we Christians insist is a part of our creed, regardless as to how young he might be, the death of a fellow worker, would be an occasion for rejoicing. Fully aware that no one can turn off his emotion of grief at will, it should be noted that our reaction to death is usually rather pagan. The body of the deceased is dressed and groomed so as to look like it is only asleep. Friends and relatives are welcome to view the corpse and express their condolences. And those who pay their respects speak consistently in the past tense. Expressions like: "He *was* a good man . . . She *had* many friends . . .Everybody *loved* him . . . She *made* a lasting impression on the community" all bespeak the world's resignation to the finality of physical death. To talk in the present tense about one who has died surprises most people who stand around a funeral parlor. Anyone who tries such an experiment will discover that he is quickly shunned as though such talk makes him suspect as an unrealistic, religious fanatic.

In reality, what happens at the death of a Christian is a glorious thing. One is promoted from a lower to a higher position of service. To the loyal servants in the parable of the talents, the master says, "Well done, good and faithful servant, thou hast been faithful over a few things, I will make thee ruler over many things" (Matthew 25:21). Throughout the Bible is found the assuring certainty that the world beyond is an advancement over this world and an improvement upon it. The Christian is honored and promoted at death.

Were any of us to object to the promotion of a friend in his field of labor on the earth, in all likelihood that person would be jealous. Various reasons might be put forward, but underlying each of them would be an envious nature. The employer who grants the promotion has a legitimate right to question his own decision, but not a fellow worker. Likewise, the Lord is entitled to advance whom He will and the rest of us are in no position to complain. Is it possible that we are envious of the victory won when we object to another's death? That may strike us as unreasonable, although in the substratum of the unconscious it may be clearly the case.

To protest a promotion granted to one who is young on the job may seem to have more validity than to object to the advancement of one with seniority. The younger person does not have the experience or the years of service normally assumed necessary for the added responsibility. Nevertheless, the employer is the judge in such matters and has the prerogative of making the decision. So God cannot be impugned as unjust when a younger Christian dies. He who sees, what the rest of us do not, always does what is right. That is part of what it means to be God. To be God means to have the wisdom and the power to overrule man in his foolish inadequacy.

One of the finest, most gracious and loyal women in our church was quite suddenly called to her eternal home following a double surgery that overtaxed her heart. In her middle 50s, she was charming and radiant in her faith and literally loved by everybody. For several years she had been on the church staff as financial secretary and her task was done to perfection. On the night of her death, her brokenhearted husband sat with me as he wrestled with his grief and the shock of his wife's early departure. Almost with a nervous chuckle in his voice he said, "Maybe God needed a bookkeeper in heaven and that is why she died." Without hesitation came my own understanding reply, "If that is what He needed, then He picked the best!" No one knows whether the Lord needs bookkeepers. The New Testament does suggest that He keeps records on us. But the fact remains that God gives promotions to those who most deserve them. And He alone has the knowledge and right to make that decision.

Some Finish Their Work Sooner

When the disciples tried to deter Christ from returning to Bethany where recently some had sought to stone Him, He replied with a most interesting statement, "Are there not twelve hours in the day? If anyone walks in the day, he does not stumble, because he sees the light of this world" (John 11:9). By these words the followers of Jesus learned that He was sure of divine providence. While there was work to do in the world no harm could come to Him. Livingstone was saying the same thing when he wrote, "I am immortal till my work is done." If this is true, then he who is in Christ by faith cannot die too soon. God will complete His work in us for this world before we die. This may mean that He will have to accelerate it as did the Master when He speeded up the process of making wine from water at Cana in Galilee (John 2:1-11). How it is done is the Father's business, not man's. Of course, no one should take this deference to the sovereignty of God to mean that anyone's work is *fully* done in this world. The Christian's work will continue through all eternity. This fact is more than encouraging to those who feel shortchanged by death, who feel like one's life is cut off before its task is completed. When viewed in the light of eternity, only a part of that task is to be completed here, but that part has been done to completion when death comes.

In the Jerusalem Talmud is a story about Rabbi Bun bar Hijja, a beloved scholar who died at an early age in the first half of the fourth century after Christ. Many of his tutors from former days came to honor his passing. The remarks given by Rabbi Ze'era were worked into a parable similar to one told earlier by Jesus (Matthew 20:1-16). A king hired several laborers to work for him. One of them proved to be so much more industrious than the others that the king soon pulled him off the job and spent the rest of the day just walking and conversing with him. When wages were paid at the close of the day everybody received the same amount. Some complained because they had worked all day and the other laborer had spent only two hours on the job. The king explained that he had done no injustice to anyone since the one laborer had done more in two hours than any of the others had done during the whole day. And the eloquent funeral oration concluded with the suggestion that Rabbi Bun bar Hijja had accomplished more in his brief 28 years than many aged scholars had done in a century. Thus God had called home the one whose task was done. It should be discerned by each of us that the Lord does not pay by the hour but by the job.

Could the mission of Christ on the earth have been performed more completely if He had not died at 33? Had He lived longer, what more could have been done? Assuredly, more lame persons could have been healed and more lepers could have been cleansed; more blind men might have had their sight restored and more demented minds could have been touched by the Master's integrating hand. But the purpose for which He came was to redeem mankind from the curse and the crucifixion was a vital part of that mission. Had He lived in the flesh to be 1,000, nothing could have been added to His perfect atonement for sin. He said as much Himself when, on the cross, the dying Savior exclaimed, "It is finished" (John 19:30). Only 33 years, but the Lord's earthly task was completed and He was ready to go home. Since it is hard for us to see why our loved ones must die so young, even as it was for Mary and the close friends of Jesus, we must have the spiritual perception which only grace can give. An unnamed poet speaks with great insight and strong faith when he affirms for everyone having suffered through the death of a young companion or friend:

> They pass from work to greater work
> Who rest before their noon,
> Ah, God is very good to them,
> They do not die too soon.

That is a much better way of looking at one of life's puzzling enigmas than is the often heard querulous and complaintive attitude.

Further Testing Would Be Counterproductive

If the Scriptures are correct in stating that the Lord does not permit us to be tempted beyond our breaking point, would it not be just as logical to say that He does not allow us to be tested unnecessarily? When our lives have been adequately disciplined and our faithfulness has been sufficiently proved, is there any reason why we should not be placed in the highest echelons of divine service? And where could that be except in heaven? To ask one to conceive of

God's subjecting man unmercifully to more and more tests, when his commitment has already been refined, is to ask that one think of the Creator as a tyrant who plays with man's integrity. To keep the steel in the fire after it has been tempered is to destroy its usefulness.

There are some gentle souls who are not at home in a world like ours. It might be said that they are too good for this earth. That is probably why Enoch was translated at such an early age. For such people to be exposed to the frightening and ghastly developments evidenced after their death, might have been more than they could take. Like the steel in the fire, too much of it would have taken the life out of them. If the Creator knows how to temper the wind to the shorn lamb, He must also subject man to what his individual temperament can stand and no more. The psalmist comes to our support again, "As a father pitieth his children, so the Lord pitieth them that fear him. For he knoweth our frame; he remembereth that we are dust" (Psalm 103:13-14).

This world is a training school, not a torture chamber. The Lord is not interested in making the earthly pilgrimage a demoralizing and devastating nightmare. To allow our destruction from an overdose of temptation, persecution, or plain suffering could not be an ingredient in the divine prescription for life and health. Death in youth, if all the ramifications were known, is probably the kindest of all possibilities from a purely human standpoint. From the perspective of God, it is not just kind. It is good, and loving, and right.

Just a few years ago my own wife died rather suddenly at the age of 39 after a seven-week bout with inoperable cancer. At the time, none of us in the family could see any reason for it. With three young children to rear, it was the worst time to die. However, she was one of those gentle souls, and some of the events that transpired following her death would have been more pernicious for her spirit than lymphosarcoma was for her body. There is good reason to believe that someday she will tell me that my surmise was right. Further testing would have been needless. She had fought a good fight, kept the faith, and won her right to an early death. Having quickly completed her earthly task, she was admitted to an enlarged realm of love and service, where that which had been begun would be continued.

Bishop Badley of the Methodist Episcopal Church of North India tells of one of his sons who, soon after completing his university course, became ill and died. He had been preparing to return to India as a missionary, but his life had been prematurely cut off. All the training was for naught since he would not be able to use it in the service of God. Then one night the Lord spoke to Bishop Badley saying, "I am using your son on this side!"

Could any one of us get a glimpse of what our loved ones are doing in paradise, we would be amazed beyond anything we might imagine.

A Word about the Unbeliever

Not every person who dies young is a committed Christian. Naturally, the question arises as to why death should come so soon to them. If it is correct to say that no Christian dies too soon, provided his death is seen in an eternal perspective, would it not be reasonable to presume that the same thing can be stated about the non-believer? If the Christian's earthly work is done, then so is that of the non-Christian. The difference is not in this life where all of us are given ample time to complete whatever we are going to do. Most of us could finish our task much sooner if we applied ourselves, as did Jesus, to eternal priorities with consuming dedication. The difference lies in whether we are going to continue with God or without Him in the world beyond.

God does not predestine some to be saved and some to be lost. Spurgeon used to pray, "O God, save the elect, and elect some more." Salvation is offered to all people and no one is shut out by God. Only one way is known by which one can be shut off from the Lord. That is, by closing the door himself. An early death is no more apt to cancel our chances of redemption than a later one. Acceptance in the life to come is determined by personal faith in Christ as Savior and Lord, not by works. Unquestionably, He who predestines none to be lost, but has perfect foreknowledge, will not permit the death of anyone as long as there is the remotest possibility of his being redeemed. We may quite safely presume that there is nothing accidental about man's death. No unbeliever dies young unless the all-wise God knows that further prolongation of human existence would not alter his choice or destiny. This is not predestination. It is divine omniscience. God has predestined all of us for salvation, but He has predetermined no one.

Getting one's job done on the earth is determined not by his being a Christian, but by his capacity for a task which in turn is determined by the kind of life he has chosen. Man may complete his earthly work as either a Christian or a non-Christian. The work will be totally different depending on his choice, but in either case it will be completed at death. He who lives and dies without Christ will find that his full contribution has been made in a fleeting human pilgrimage.

159

His contribution will be in the past. There will be no further opportunity to add to or expand that work in another dimension. In other words, he will have no future. On the other hand, he who lives and dies in Christ will discover his completed earthly task amplified with new and undreamed of possibilities for continuation in the coming kingdom.

Chapter 10

The Final Exam

The Unavoidable Decision

Life would be much easier if we did not have to make decisions. It would also be colorless. Without the discipline of decision making, man would be a jellyfish. Being under compulsion to weigh the pros and cons of alternate positions and actions creates a climate of responsibility. Making rational choices is basic to the business of living. Since the first days of Adam and Eve the human race has been compelled to exist decisively. Human existence makes little or no sense at all unless we have a part in shaping it. If men are irresponsible, their lives are shaped without their will. In responsible decision alone does one share with the Creator Himself in creative living.

Some decisions are more important than others. And the more important they are the harder becomes the matter of making up one's mind. Among us, of course, are those who fret and fume away all their days because they cannot come to a final decision about anything, great or small. A court order is necessary before such persons can say whether the breakfast eggs are to be scrambled or fried. Everybody in the family is dragged into the problem before they settle on what dress or tie to wear to a simple open house at the local day care center. But there are much graver problems facing us than that. We may not know it, but it is true.

Procrastination is human nature's built in way of getting around a clear yes or no. The longer we can delay nailing down a hard and fast decision, the easier we feel. But nobody is fooled by this, certainly not ourselves. Though the time must come for facing the situation squarely, it is not here yet. So we straddle the fence as long as we can get by with it. My young son, Andy, used to enjoy maneuvering his dad into promising him the things he wanted. Discovering that these promises were often made while watching television or reading a book, it became necessary to be a bit more cautious. Henceforth the response came to be *maybe*. One day he sobered me by saying quite seriously, "Don't say maybe, say yes or no. Maybe is in between." No one likes in-betweenness.

What we despise most in Pontius Pilate is his weakness as he interrogated Jesus on the night of the trial. Often the governor of Judea had been called on to decide important political matters. Never before had a situation of such enormous consequence involved him in the court procedure as his encounter with the Stranger of Galilee. It was too much for his feet of clay. Face to face with God and he could not decide what to do! We might feel sorry for him if he had been a bit more of a man, but he was a coward and no one feels sympathy for that kind of fellow. Vacillating, wavering like a leaf in the wind, the political puppet could not bring himself to admit the innocence of Christ by standing with Him against the pious, murderous priests. Neither had he the courage to side with the priests against the Lord. Instead, Pilate defended his own innocence in remaining neutral, in choosing neither side in a religious quarrel that was outside his domain. Rather than judge on the basis of a lack of evidence against Jesus and send the accusers home with a stern rebuke, the governor asked that motley mob of prejudiced priests and bribed barbarians to decide the issue for him. "What shall I do with Jesus who is called the Christ?" he asked (Matthew 27:22). It was not as though the crowd was an impartial jury anxious to hear the facts. They had made up their minds before the trial began and they wanted the death penalty. When it was evident that there was insufficient strength of character within him to reject the demand for Christ's crucifixion, he dramatically washed his hands and insisted that what was about to happen was not in any way his responsibility. A dastardly deed it was, and Pilate knew it.

No matter what Pilate may have thought or coerced himself into believing against his better judgment, Jesus Christ will not be washed off one's hands so easily. Crowding in on every side, this Son of God is unavoidable. He will not be evaded nor can anyone remain neutral toward Him. History's most disturbing person is this Man from Nazareth. It was not He who was on trial that night in Judea; rather it was the governor and the people themselves who were taking the final exam. And they failed it.

Daily Quizzes and Mid-Terms

In keeping with the analogy of life as a training school, we would expect some method of checking up on us on a regular, almost daily basis. An earlier chapter has dealt with periodic exams quite extensively, but a further word must be included here. The daily quizzes are established for the purpose of determining whether we are keeping up with our work, whether the particular day has added anything to our storehouse of experienced knowledge about God's ways with man. Failure on any one or several of these pop quizzes does not destroy one's hope of passing the course, though they do figure into the overall quality point standing of the student of life.

Not even the mid-terms (or the larger segment exams which come from time to time to test us more severely) such as illness, grief, or financial loss are a finalized criterion for deciding failure. Being yet human everyone shows up rather poorly on most of these exams. Very few manage to meet all the testings of life with an unblemished record. Some are able to face serious sickness in great confidence while the threat of unemployment breaks them out in a cold sweat. Some are not much disturbed by financial problems but dwell in constant anxiety about the day when a parent or a spouse may die. When what has been so dreaded finally happens, they get through it but the score on their exam is not the kind which makes them proud.

As the last rays of the sun set on Friday of Holy Week the disciples went into seclusion. In spite of all Jesus had taught and shown them, they were still not capable of handling His departure from their world. Not a shred of evidence can be found to suggest that any one of them was filled with optimism or had even a shred of hope that the tragedy they faced would turn out all right. There was only despair, disillusionment, defeat. They were afraid of the priests and disappointed with Jesus. The fact of a coming resurrection did not enter their heads, and yet the Master had carefully prepared them for this hour. Two thousand years this side of the cross we cannot imagine how they so completely missed it, but then we have the advantage of the years and see in retrospective what they could not perceive in anticipation. Every disciple miserably failed the examination given on the eve of the Jewish Sabbath.

The Final Is Final

The nature of a final exam that makes it dead serious is its finality. There are no exams given beyond the final. And it is referred to by this name not solely because it comes at the end but also because it reveals the whole story and terminates opportunity. Other lesser exams must be seen in the light of this all important determinative. It is one thing to keep pace with the daily requirements and take life in little chunks. And that is crucially important to peace of mind or personal contribution. But it is another thing to have all the chunks covered in one all-inclusive examination. That is what the final is all about.

Recognizing that knowledge is necessary in taking any tests, the man who stands before the testings in the university of human existence is extremely aware of the underlying indispensable nature of experience. It is here the final is geared to separate the men from the boys, to reveal how one's knowledge has been related to experience. The term *experience* is a significant one in every area of man's relationships, but nowhere is it more crucial than in his relationship to God. We must never forget that it is not a mastery of content in the school of knowledge that is basic, but the establishing of a relationship with the Creator and Redeemer through personal experience. Job came to see this toward the end of his vast suffering when he exclaimed, "I have heard of thee by the hearing of the ear, but now mine eye seeth thee" (Job 42:5). At last he had experienced God, and the relationship altered his whole perception. Knowing God is not the same thing as knowing about Him.

For Moses the major test came at the beginning of his work as emancipator of his people from Egyptian bondage. Precisely at that moment, when he stood before the burning bush and heard the Lord God speak to him, did Moses experience God. Beyond the least shadow of a doubt, his whole life was changed for time and for eternity in the new relatedness which came to him while tending the sheep in Midian.

For Noah the test came when the Lord came to him with instructions for building an ark. For Abraham, it was when the covenant was given. For Jacob, the final was taken at Peniel. In each of these historical instances, the final and eternally determinative exam was passed or failed depending on the individual's faith or lack of it in the God who called him.

Progressively, the Father in heaven had revealed Himself to men as they were able to comprehend divine love and redemption. When His people were ready for the incarnate presence of the Lord, Jesus was born. Since that day of Christ's death and resurrection the entire world is subjected to its final exam in an inescapable encounter with the living Lord. Individual man passes or fails the big one on the basis of personal faith in and commitment to Jesus the Christ. To stand at the judgment at the end of time and succumb to failure, will mean one thing and only one thing. It will mean that one has not related his knowledge to an experienced encounter with and commitment to the Son of God.

Some have taken their final exam early in life as did Samuel (1 Samuel 3) and some quite late as did the dying thief (Luke 23:39-43). Regardless as to when it happens there is no way to evade it, to cut out and spare ourselves the real reckoning with God about our sins. He who accepts Christ by faith here has already been judged for sin and acquitted. But even though we know by faith that we have passed, there is a sense in which every man must yet hear the Lord say so when the Book of Life is opened on that day toward which all creation moves (Revelation 20:12). The presence of our names in the Lamb's Book of Life will be the evidence needed to prove that we have passed the final.

None Can Take the Course Again

A growing number of churchmen are speculating about a second chance, another opportunity after death. Our humaneness is enough to tempt us to read this theory into the picture. Nowhere are we given sanction for this idea in the words of Jesus or anywhere else in the New Testament. To insist on another chance after death is nothing other than rationalization on human reason alone. Were the pagans who die without hearing the gospel to be given opportunity to hear and respond in the world to come, it would not be a second chance. It would be only the first. But we are not even promised that this will be the case, though we can be certain that the Lord will handle such a situation with justice and mercy. We are primarily interested here in those who have heard and rejected the gospel offer. For them there is no second chance to take the exam and believe.

Eastern religions have influenced many thinkers within the Christian Church who are hinting the probability of reincarnation. This would be more than a second opportunity to take all the daily quizzes and mid-terms again, to relive one's life with prospects for improvement. Flirtation with pagan philosophies is very dangerous and we must insist that there is no warrant for this seductive theory in the Bible. If one could take the full course over, including all the exams, then what would have been the purpose in this life at all? We might as well have not lived. This existence has meaning only because it counts for something eternally significant.

Likewise, it should be clearly stated that we have no biblical authority for expecting some intermediate state between this world and the next where the dross will be consumed and the gold refined. The refining process takes place here and now as we have already discussed in a previous section of this book. The rich man asked for a chance to have his sentence lightened by a visit from Lazarus. In the world of the damned, one is hardly in a position to ask favors of God. He was not given a chance to go back to the earth and make adjustments in the life he could live nor was he encouraged to believe that the tortures of *Hades* would be renewing or rehabilitative for his spirit (Luke 16:1-9). The entire book of Revelation insists that death seals man's chances. To argue otherwise is to build a theological system on a premise that is man-made and foreign to the scriptural account.

No Proxy Arrangement Is Made

Since the days of Adam and Eve, both of whom tried to shift the responsibility on to someone else, man has attempted to substitute the exam of someone other than himself. At times it is a saintly mother or father whom a son or daughter counts on to get them by the judgment. Even priests and pastors have been used unknowingly as a proxy for someone in the parish. College students have been known to take exams for one another in situations where the crowds allowed individuals to be overlooked. The judgment day on a university campus may be filled with inequities because the judge is as human as are the students. At the judgment of all men in the world to come, things will be different. There no one is a number and none is overlooked. Each man's record will have been perfectly kept and personal names will be known. The reason for the difference is that the Judge is divine.

The old-time religion may have been good enough for father, but if it is to be good enough for me, it will have to be a part of my life and not just a pious feeling that wells up in my heart at the thought of father's vital piety. He cannot take my exam. It is not allowed. No one would eat in a restaurant and ignore the check because his father happens to eat there. No one expects to be safe from an epidemic on the strength of his father's immunity. No one imagines that the commissioner of internal revenue will overlook his unpaid taxes since his father's were paid in full. And yet these same intelligent people expect the divine judgment to take care of itself because they were born in a Christian home, attended a Christian Church, or were reared in a nominally Christian land.

Man is more foolish than he ought to be if he thinks that another can stand up for him when the roll is called up yonder. The songwriter was expressing a biblical truth when he added the personal note, "I'll be there!" Indeed, every man must take his own exam while here on the earth and confront his own record at the final bar of justice. It is one thing to anticipate being *up yonder* as a time of wonderful joy, but it is another thing to recognize that each one of us will have to stand there on our own two feet and give an account of the life we have lived. To the church at Rome, Paul wrote, "We shall all stand before the judgment seat of God; for it is written, As I live, says the Lord, every knee shall bow to me, and every tongue shall give praise to God. So each of us shall give account of himself to God" (Romans 14:10-12).

The Master Key

Whether we students of life pass the exam and are accepted in the coming Kingdom will be decided on how our response to God compares with the master key. Usually, examinations are checked against a master answer sheet. Unless the two are the same the student fails. So it is with the Lord's standard of judgment. The master key by which He checks our lives is Jesus Christ. Paul reminds us that "if any one is in Christ, he is a new creation" (2 Corinthians 5:17 NIV), that is, he is recreated into the image of God which was marred by the fall of Adam. As man enters into union with the Son of God who redeems, he conquers with Christ the son of God who rebels. At that moment he "puts on the Lord Jesus Christ" (Romans 13:14), a synonymous analogy with being "in Christ". The apostle even talks about being "crucified with Christ" and yet living in Him (Galatians 2:20). All this is another way of saying that man has passed his final exam when he finds his true identity in the Savior, when his response to God is directly related to the Redeemer's life and work.

In summarizing His remarks about life's final exam in the conversation with Nicodemus, Jesus succinctly states the heart of the gospel: "For God so loved the world that he gave his only begotten Son, that whoever believes in him should not perish but have eternal life. For God sent his Son into the world, not to condemn the world, but that the world might be saved through him. He who believes in him is not condemned; he who does not believe is condemned already, because he has not believed in the name of the only Son of

God" (John 3:16-18 NKJV). Christ is the answer. That is not a simplistic solution that is inadequate for a complicated world. He is the master key, the right and only answer to man's exam. Unless our answer on the final coincides with the Lord's answer on the cross, then we fail. And that failure, once earthly life is over, is irremediable and eternal. Our Lord specifically states that He is "the door of the sheep" (John 10:7) and finalizes that truth when He says to Thomas, "I am the way, and the truth, and the life; no one comes to the Father, but by me" (John 14:6 RSV).

There are many good answers to life's final exam, but only one which is correct. Jesus Christ is that answer. Man, in his unregenerate attempts at saving himself, has come forth with some excellent ideas. Even the church has been seduced by the world to try the ways of men. The trouble with these good answers to the enigma of life is that they do not work. And regardless as to how reasonable, logical, and acceptable to us they appear, such answers are of no consequence before God. Reason without faith can land us in hell, a hell no less damning because of our intellectual acumen. While faith does not necessarily contradict human reason (when that reason is unbiased in its search for truth) one may egotistically rationalize himself into a self-sufficient failure before God. Faith, more than reason (if there is an imbalance possible), is the answer. This is why the wise old sage pens, "There is a way that seems right to a man, but its end is the way to death" (Proverbs 14:12 RSV) and why the prophet foresees Christ's day and hears Him saying, "This is the way, walk in it" (Isaiah 30:21 RSV). It is beyond dispute that "he who does not enter the sheepfold by the door (Christ) but climbs in by another way, that man is a thief and a robber" (John 10:1 RSV).

Faith and Commitment

From Egypt to Canaan had been a long, trying journey for the Hebrews under the leadership of Moses and Joshua. After 40 years (a needless delay caused by faithlessness and disobedience) the people waged war against the inhabitants of the land promised to Abraham and marched into their new home. When the time of Joshua's death drew near, the great warrior gathered all the Israelites at Shechem and confronted them with a decision. He recounted the mighty deeds of Jehovah in rescuing them from bondage and giving them victory over the Amorites. Then, on the basis of the Lord's goodness, Joshua challenged the Hebrews to "put away the gods" that had been served by their fathers in their times of apostasy and serve the Lord of Israel. In the event that they were unwilling to serve Jehovah, their dying leader demanded that they make up their minds about where their loyalties would lie. "Choose you this day whom ye will serve, whether the gods which your fathers served which were on the other side of the river, or the gods of the Amorites, in whose land ye dwell; but as for me and my house, we will serve the Lord" (Joshua 24:14-15).

In every man's life there comes a time for decision. It came to the nation of Israel and to each individual member of it. It came to Pontius Pilate. It comes to us. We are compelled to make a choice. Either we will choose the gods of the world of human sufficiency or we will commit ourselves to the Father of our Lord Jesus Christ. There is no alternative. Neutrality is by its very nature a decision against the Lord. Masses of the world's people are "in the valley of decision" (Joel 3:14), and there is no exit from it until a choice is made.

Joshua seems emphatic enough in his insistence that living in the land of promise demands faith in God and commitment to Him. That is obviously true whether we are speaking of the covenant relationship between the Lord and the nation or of the new covenant made with us in the blood of Christ. It is further true whether we are referring to the land of promise here or the one that is yet to come. Heaven buds here on the earth in the hearts of men and women who know and serve Christ, and it blossoms into full bloom when the saints of God are received into the eternal habitations either at death or at the second coming of Jesus.

Faith and commitment are brought together in one concise word in the letter to the Romans: "If you confess with your lips that Jesus is Lord and believe in your heart that God raised him from the dead, you will be saved. For man believes with his heart and so is justified, and he confesses with his lips and so is saved" (Romans 10:9-10 RSV). To confess Christ, not just with the lips but with the whole heart, is what commitment is all about. To believe that the Father in heaven has raised Jesus from the dead is to have faith that justifies. It is to admit the deity and redemptive power of the Lord. And when this justifying faith is coupled with a life of commitment the result is salvation. The final exam will be passed in no other known way. Efforts to find a way around such ultimate examination have been undertaken by the human race since the beginning of time. By now we ought to know that there are no detours or shortcuts.

Repentance and Conversion

These two words, repentance and conversion, are nearly forgotten in the vocabulary of the Church. But they are still biblical and they are both at the center of the final examination of every individual. To have faith and make a commitment are beginning steps in the divine answer for man's sin. Out of this beginning must evolve a conversion of the individual from self and sin to God and righteousness. To the people who had crowded into Solomon's Porch on the occasion of the healing of the lame man, Simon Peter exclaimed, "Repent . . . and be converted, that your sins may be blotted out" (Acts 3:19).

When a man repents, he changes his mind. When he is converted, he changes his behavior. The two belong together and must not be separated. One may repent without changing his life as in the case of Judas Iscariot (Matthew 27:8). True repentance is godly sorrow that issues in godly living. Repentance is a necessity if one is to find life. Jesus requires it of all, not just the worst offenders against God. "Unless you repent," He says, "you will all likewise perish" (Luke 13:5). But conversion is a necessity also. This same Jesus clearly states, "Unless you turn and become like children, you will never enter the kingdom of heaven" (Matthew 18:3 RSV).

In repentance a person intellectually, as well as emotionally, turns away from the former attitudes that motivated him in an existence of self-will and ego glory. At the moment of repentance he stops trying to pass the final in his own strength and wisdom. Suddenly he realizes that to continue in his humanistic efforts to find an answer to life is like one beating his head against a wall to acquire intelligence. But such a person is likely to despair if he stops with repentance, a recognition that his prior manner of life has been useless and bad. Repentance alone can be terribly crippling. Therefore, conversion is a vital ingredient in this exam.

If repentance is a turning from something, conversion is a turning to something else. Thus conversion implies an acceptance of the answer of God for which all our earlier substitutes have been as nothing. It is a change of one's life and conduct growing out of an honest look at past failure in the idolizing of self. And to do this, the beginnings of faith and personal commitment to which we have referred above are called into play. Faith in the redeeming Christ as man's only hope, commitment to Him as Lord and Savior, and conversion to a new behavior in Jesus Christ—these sum up the qualifying facets of life's final exam.

Chapter 11

When The Grades Are In

Someone Must Keep Score

Even so transient a thing as a game needs a scorekeeper. Perhaps the players themselves will keep tab on one another, depending on the importance attached to the game itself, but somebody is delegated to watch for points made and to enter them on the permanent record. At times the same person will serve as a kind of check on cheating while keeping the score card itself. In more significant games, other persons are designated as referees or umpires to watch for infractions of the rules, unintentional fouls, and other similar involvements or movements disallowed by the book of regulations. Without the keeping of a score there is no meaning to the game at all and no one has any idea how he has performed in the competition. Scoring is an imperative unless the game is no more than a bit of silly fun. Of course, silly fun has its place in life, but it is hardly to be classed in the same category with more formalized sports.

It is not uncommon for life to be called a game. Caution must be exercised at this point lest such a concept allow us to take a lighthearted approach to our existence. From the idea of a game, which has some merit, it is easy to degenerate into a completely unmerited image of life as a game of fools' play. If this is what is meant by human existence's being a game, then the world needs to be divested of a false analogy. Man's earthly existence is much too serious ever to be taken lightly. It is of such grave import as to deserve the underscoring of every event.

Could we keep a proper perspective on the seriousness of life, we would be safe in the use of the game analogy. In the more exalted sense of the word, almost everything is a game. This is so whether the subject under consideration is athletics, business, education, politics, or religion. All of these top priorities include competition, regulations, fair play, penalty, scoring, and victory or defeat. Under no circumstances can any segment of man's life be meaningful without something similar to a score's being maintained. And, if nowhere else, that score is being recorded in the individual's conscience deep down in the non-molecular make up of his total being.

No one would have any way to check on himself if a score were not entered in the ledger of his days and years. Without this arrangement, there would be little chance of knowing where one is, at the moment, in relation to his point of beginning and future goal. Progress and regression can be measured only as a person reads his present level of attainment through a transparent overlay of his past history and coming objectives. Thus scoring is an essential.

Always there are some among us who refuse to look at themselves. They convince themselves that as long as they do not see too clearly where their attitudes and deeds have brought them or where their direction is leading them, there is no need for alarm. Deliberately, the effort is made to cover up. Either they hide their score or cheat in an attempt to make the record look better. Regardless as to which choice is made, no one is deceived except the man who faces his own life dishonestly. Certainly, "God is not mocked, for whatever a man sows, that he will also reap" (Galatians 6:7). The Creator keeps track of the score whether we do or not. Nothing is concealed from Him who sees all things and judges wisely. It is to man's advantage if he recognizes this fact early and seeks to keep his own score card as accurately and unprejudiced as does God.

Progressive and Future Judgment

Multitudes insist that judgment day is now. Talk of a day of judgment at the end of the age is for these people both unlikely and unrealistic. Life has its own judgment ingrained right in its fabric and each man pays for his errors as he daily moves and breathes. It is entirely pay as you go. Nothing is reserved for the future. There is no final showdown when people will be faced with a lifetime of sin. So runs the argument and it sounds plausible. It sounds that way because it is at least partially right.

Judgment is a present experience. Man does have to face the deeds and attitudes of his existence daily. And judgment is progressive, too. That is, it keeps coming up and the weight of past guilt feelings seems to cling to us across the years. With some people, the burden of guilt and failure gets so heavy that they take the easy way out. They shoot themselves or take an overdose of sleeping pills. After all, if judgment is confined to this life, why not end it all when things get too difficult? That would be the sensible thing to do. Perhaps far more persons resist the temptation to commit suicide than succumb to it simply because they are afraid that the "this world judgment only" people are wrong.

At a previous point in this book, some discussion was offered about judgment for the believer in Christ. Let us repeat here that judgment day is now if we know what we are saying. The believer is already judged in Christ, his substitute. The coming judgment on sin is only for the unbeliever. And even then there is a sense in which that day will be only a confirmation of what the unregenerate knows even now. Thus, judgment day is now if this is what is implied by the present tense frame of reference. Already we are judged either in Christ or outside Him. What the individual knows himself to be at the end time will be made public forever.

In the more balanced view of judgment, it can be observed that it is neither progressive nor future but both. It is both this-worldly and other-worldly, both temporal and eternal, both continuously now and terminally then. Lest there develop a misunderstanding of this whole matter of judgment, however, it must be noted that two judgment days are mentioned in the Bible and, while concerned with different matters entirely, are both progressive and future. More shall be said about this twofold judgment as we proceed in coming sections of this study.

Nothing to Do with Passing Or Failing

The scorecard has no relationship whatsoever to the believer's salvation. Our deliverance from the power and domination of sin is not a matter for keeping score. Salvation by works is a damnable doctrine nowhere supported by the Scriptures. The whole Protestant Church, with all its splintered branches, grew directly out of a brave protest against a much abused understanding of salvation. According to the ancient Church, the human race will be saved by faith in the death and resurrection of Jesus Christ. If any man is lost, it will be due to his rejection of the offer of divine grace. Works are futile to render one justified before God. Unless the roots are right the fruits will be wrong no matter how attractive might be their appearance.

Gradually, across the passing centuries, the institutional church had grown powerful, gigantic and corrupt. Unenlightened masses of people were held in bondage to an ecclesiastical giant which bled them to death of all their energies and possessions with the promise of eternal life as payment. The clergy and monks themselves were duped into believing that their good works and austerities would merit the favor of the Lord. With this salvation by works doctrine uppermost in the minds of the people, man slaved and sacrificed in abject misery in hope that someday God would be appeased and the assurance of salvation would be obtained. Luther was right in leading a revolt which broke the shackles of the people and led them into a fresh understanding of the biblical truth of salvation by faith alone.

Since works, which are seen by others, are not the criteria by which God decides who passes on the final exam, none of us can presume to be able to judge another's acceptance or rejection before the Eternal. Only God can do that because only He is all knowing. A Kentucky father lost two sons in the Civil War, one in the Union Blue and the other in the Confederate Gray. On the stone over their double grave, he inscribed: "Only God knows which was right". Likewise, only the eternal and wise Judge of all the earth knows who among us has believed and who has not. It is His perfect knowledge of our faith or dis-faith in the gift of

His Son upon the cross which will determine every man's passing or failing. Grades on the scorecard have nothing to do with that. It is critical that we get this crystal clear in our heads if we are going to begin to comprehend the judgment in its over all implications.

Position in the Class

In every graduating class there are some who are in the bottom half and some who are in the upper half of the group. Most of them would be deemed average students, a few below and a few above average. A select group would graduate *cum laude* and an even more select few would complete their schooling *magna* or *summa cum laude*. Each person who passed the finals would be among the graduates, but not all of them would have equal standing. The class prophet is wise if he considers the levels of achievement in making his predictions. Often such prophecy does not materialize because the prophet, as well as the graduate, is short sighted and conditioned by the future of human existence on an imperfect planet. On graduation day at the end of the age, there will be no such discrepancies since every man's life will be seen in the true light of eternity.

Scores are being tabulated even now to be brought to light at the judgment of works. Every man must stand before the bar of justice and receive his reward. The reward may be good or it may be bad. Any reward received by the redeemed will be good even as any reward received by the unbeliever will be bad. In both heaven and hell, however, there will be levels of recompense. The person with the highest payment in hell will have the lightest eternal punishment. By the same token, the one receiving the lowest payment in heaven will have the lightest eternal glory. But the lowest rank in heaven will be far superior to the highest rank in hell. The difference will lie in one thing—not what our level or reward may or may not be, but Who it is that we are destined to dwell with and serve forever. Can any conceive the vast difference between communion with Christ (even if there were no reward at all for works) and existence with Satan (though in the most superior rank) for all eternity? Probably not. But we all know that heaven will still be heaven and hell will still be hell regardless as to the degrees of compensation. Hell, by its simplest definition, is separation from God who is the source of life. There can be no punishment more severe than that.

Once admitted into heaven on the basis of our faith in and commitment to Jesus Christ, there remains the simple task of finding where each person belongs in that world and what shall be his place of service. And once received into hell on the basis of our lack of faith and commitment, there begins the classifying of the unregenerate into their places of punishment. Those in hell will have failed on the final exam, though some degree of human goodness within them deserves and will receive consideration. Those in heaven will have passed on the final exam and their position in the class will be decided at the judgment for works.

This is clearly enunciated by the skillful words of the writer of the letter to the Corinthians: "Now if anyone builds on the foundation [Christ Jesus] with gold, silver, precious stones, wood, hay, or stubble, each man's work will become manifest; for the Day will disclose it, because it will be revealed with fire, and the fire will test what sort of work each one has done. If the work which any man has built on the foundation survives, he will receive a reward. If any man's work is burned up, he will suffer loss, though he himself will be saved, but only as through fire" (1 Corinthians 3: 12-15 RSV). Paul is here explaining degrees of reward for the Christian, but we may safely assume that the same criteria for levels of punishment in hell will be employed.

Manifestly, Paul is talking here about the day of judgment for works, not the judgment for sin, which holds no fear for the believer who has full benefits of deliverance through the cross of Christ. He is dogmatic about the indestructibility of the right foundation. And he is sure that what happens to the severe test of man's works will not guarantee or annul his hope of eternal life. Pointedly, the apostle notes the descending scale of works from symbolic gold to symbolic stubble. All this obviously means that there is such a thing as being genuinely saved here and hereafter and still losing one's reward.

It All Adds Up

Here is where all those daily quizzes and mid-terms figure into the picture. None of them will be overlooked. Our reward or lack of it will be in direct ratio to those day by day tests of our growth and service. "For the Son of man is to come with his angels in the glory of his Father, and then he will repay every man for what he has done" (Matthew 16:27 RSV). We may be rather certain that the rewards will be given for everything from deeds of personal and social kindness to sincere and heartfelt piety. It is to be granted that Jesus was making particular reference to the *brethren* of the Hebrew nation when He spoke the words recorded in Matthew 25:31-46. Nevertheless, His accolades of praise will be as appropriate for a Gentile as for a Jew on that day: "I was hungry and you gave me food . . . thirsty and you gave me drink . . . sick and you visited me . . . I say to you, as you did it unto one of the least of these, my brethren, you did it to me".

Of interest is the fact that the deeds of love were done without being conscious of Christ's surveillance, certainly without knowledge of His involvement. Unquestionably, the most rewarding deeds of all are those done with no thought of praise or notice. Jesus went so far as to declare emphatically that if one seeks the applause of men for his good works, there is nothing more which he can expect (Matthew 6:2). But for him who is unassuming and uninterested in piling up credits with the public, "the Father who sees in secret will reward him" (Matthew 6:4).

Of further interest, is the word of the Lord relating to more pietistic endeavors. They apparently have their rewards, too, and God keeps a score card on them. Our Lord speaks of praying and fasting as well as aiding the needy. The Father who sees in secret will see to it that the time spent in cultivating a devotional life and disciplining one's spirit is not in vain. All kinds of rewards await all kinds of Christian devotion and service. It all adds up.

From the days of long ago comes a story which illustrates in a homespun way what is meant by the concept of degrees or reward. An affluent lady had in her domestic employ a poor woman who was always radiantly contagious in her Christian faith. She was always happy and went about her cleaning and cooking chores with singing. Never could she do enough for others and, when it came to Bible study, prayer, and church attendance, she was unsurpassed. Hardly ever could she open her mouth without praising the Lord. Her mistress secretly envied her radiance even though she did not understand her.

One night the wealthy lady dreamed of her own death. In her sleep she arrived at heaven and was warmly greeted by the keeper of the gates. What she saw was enough to take her breath away. John the revelator's description was a poor word picture for the glorious reality of the heavenly world. No earthly palace ever compared to the lavish beauty of those mansions which lined the gleaming streets of the Holy City.

When the gate keeper introduced the woman to her escort, the two of them turned in the general direction of her new home. At the outset of the walk, she called attention to the largest, most imposing edifice of them all, hoping that it might be hers. The angel only smiled and continued to walk. The farther they went the smaller grew the houses, each one reserved for some Christian. Finally, they approached what looked like the smallest cottage she had ever seen.

Stopping before the tiny quarters, the escort pointed the wealthy lady to her eternal home. Needless to say, she was puzzled and disappointed. "But whose luxurious mansion was that which we passed at the beginning of our walk?" asked the confused woman. "Ah," replied the angel, " that belongs to your wash woman. She has been sending materials up here for years by her prayers, good works, and loyal witness. If she lives much longer we will have to build on to her dwelling place." Then the angel added, "You see, my dear, the materials you sent us were so limited that this little one room cottage is the best we could do".

"Where your treasure is," said the Master, "there will your heart be also" (Matthew 6:21). God is keeping tab on us. The score is accurately entered on the record of each man's life and someday we must look it squarely in the face.

Nothing which one does for the Lord or His Kingdom here or hereafter will ever be lost. God overlooks nothing from the mightiest service to the smallest act of Christian love. Indeed, it all adds up.

The Books Will Be Open

John, in his vision of the final judgment (Revelation 20:11-15), graphically depicts a scene in which the scorecards are carefully surveyed. Those cards are called books or, what is a better rendering, scrolls. It is as if the eternal Score Keeper will roll out the complete story of each man's life with every minute detail etched in gold, gray, or black. To use another simile, it will be like watching a full length, technicolor film entitled "This Is Your Life." In some instances, the film will be delightful, while in others it will be questionable or even offensive. Nothing will be censored or cut out and there will be many surprises both good and bad. Perhaps the films at the judgment will be rated G, R, and X! If so, the rating will be a clue to one's reward.

Two sets of scrolls or books are mentioned by John. Their contents are quite different. The scrolls are distinct from the book of life. The latter contains nothing except the names of the redeemed which have been inscribed there at the moment of their acceptance of Jesus Christ by faith as Savior and Lord. To be left out of the book of life, will be to miss heaven entirely. Such an omission will be conclusive evidence requiring no further investigation. Vast numbers of people will be cast into the lake of fire on the clear evidence of this single scroll. And the omission will not be the result of some arbitrary decision by a divine court, but the direct result of man's rejection of God's way of salvation and rebellion against the divine plan of redemption.

A few years ago a supersonic Navy jet, flying at 880 miles per hour, caught up with cannon shells it had fired and shot itself down. The final judgment is the place and time when man catches up with the life he has lived and may find that it has accomplished his own ruin. The scrolls include the name of everyone who has ever lived plus the intricacies of his earthly pilgrimage. Out of these daybooks both the saved and the lost are to be evaluated. This evaluation will not determine who is to be admitted to the heavenly world and who to the demonic. The book of life settles that matter. But this evaluation of one's works will decide at what level or in what capacity he shall be permitted to exist.

Unequality and Unrest

Objections are usually met in any kind of discussion which includes a positive approach to levels of reward and degrees of punishment in the world to come. At the top of the list of objections is the fear that a distinct difference in rewarding the saints may stimulate unrest. The immediate response to this line of reasoning is that true saints always see themselves as being unworthy and over paid. These are the people who give place to others on earth; surely they will continue to do so in heaven. Furthermore, one of the coming kingdom's most pronounced blessings will be the absence of jealousy or envy. Everyone there will be fully aware that God has blessed him above his merits. No one will desire to lord it over another. Rather each will humbly desire to serve every other child of God. The level of reward will have nothing to do with dictating in earthly style to others who are one's subjects. Its only purpose will be to establish areas of service to God Himself. Unrest would be impossible in heaven. Otherwise it would not be heaven at all.

Unequality in the life to come must be distinguished from what the term implies on earth. Here unregenerate and imperfect men take advantage of superior status. There would be little problem if those in higher levels did not selfishly use their powers to make the distance between themselves and others even wider. Unequality would be of little significance if those more highly favored envisioned their blessings as opportunities for service instead of self-pampering. In heaven the nature of everyone will be inclined toward giving, not getting. We will love others more than ourselves and that is the only thing which renders unequality of no consequence. Were all of us, rich or poor, acclaimed or unsung, to honor others above self, our total world structure would be overhauled overnight and most of our interpersonal problems would be over. As hard as it is to imagine, that is the kind of world heaven will be.

Equality will be based on an entirely different concept in heaven than on earth. Were we not to point this out a vital truth would be overlooked. The basis for equality lies not in what man has done as much as in what he has believed. Let such a statement not be inferred to suggest that man can do as he pleases once he has believed. Honest faith produces works as cause and effect. We mean nothing more by the above statement than that there only two kinds of people in the world. There are sinners who have believed in the divine remedy for sin and sinners who have not. Death will not change that. For all eternity there will still be only the redeemed (sinners who accepted Christ by faith) and the unredeemed (sinners who spurned the gospel). Thus, the basic equality rests on the truth that all in heaven are alike in that they have "believed the Lord" and He has "reckoned it to them as righteousness" (Genesis 15:6).

One other word needs to be said about the need for levels of reward. Heaven will be fulfilment (more about this subject in the final chapter of this book), therefore, each man's capacity for service must be considered in direct relation to his capacity for honor. Persons capable of accomplishing more are also capable of receiving more. The larger the talent, the greater the expectation and the larger the reward. While we cannot presume that every person will do his best with what he has been given, at least we can make some sense out of the matter if we give him the benefit of the doubt. Hence, the believer with five talents would be unfulfilled unless judged and rewarded on that basis. Likewise, the believer with only one talent would be unable to receive a five talent reward. God will surely keep one's capacity for service and his faithfulness to the capacity in view as the rewards are given.

If man undertakes any comparison in heaven, it will not be between himself and another. It will be between what he was capable of by divine endowment and his personal stewardship of that trust. And even for him who has not served as well as he could (who among us has or will?), once the rewards are given and the levels established, the memory of the past with its achievements and failures will be blotted out. Thus, each one will have what he is able to joyfully handle and no one else's grade or score will seem out of line with his own.

— Chapter 12 —

Living to Die

A Universal Certainty

Every man and woman has an appointment with death. George Bernard Shaw somewhere spoke of the "ultimate statistic", that is, one out of one dies. No one is exempt. Death respects neither age, sex, race, nor creed. "It is appointed unto man once to die" (Hebrews 9:27). We spend our time, money, and energy trying to delay the appointment, but eventually it has to be kept. The poor die, and so do the rich. The good die, and so do the bad. The old die, and so do the young. The fastest growing cities in the world are the cities of the dead, the cemeteries. And their growth is permanent. The city of the dead in every community just keeps on pushing out its boundaries to include more and more. It is as if our cemeteries will not be satisfied until every person in the world is enrolled in their book of memories.

All of us know that this is true. Even so, we are artists at deception and our ingenuity is often used to fool ourselves. Few of us are willing to admit the universality of death.

Most people dislike funeral homes and funeral services. Fewer and fewer people attend funerals for their neighbors. Levi and Garfunkle were the best of friends. They were always together. When Garfunkle died a neighbor was shocked to discover that Levi was not going to attend the funeral. When asked why he would miss paying his final respects to his best friend, Levi explained, "He's not coming to my funeral so . . . I'm not going to his!" But that is not the usual reason we shun funerals. The excuse is usually that the service is conducted at a time when one cannot get off from work. Did we have all the facts, it might be discovered that most of us stay away from such events because we do not like to confront the stark reality of death. The words of the psalmist are rephrased to say, "A thousand may fall at my side, ten thousand at my right hand, but I absolutely refuse to think about it!" (Psalm 91:7). So we deny death. When someone brings up the subject, we change it. The lifeless bodies of our loved ones are not allowed to look dead. Memorial gardens are taking the place of older type cemeteries with dead looking tombstones so that we can hide the grave markers in the grass. Massive and colorful mausoleums are appearing like high rise apartments across the country to replace the grim finality associated with underground burial.

Millions have adopted the philosophy of Epicurus who said, "Where death is I am not; where I am death is not". Any such view has the disadvantage of being fully irrational and unrealistic. Reasonable people know full well that man and death are neighbors who find it in their mutual interest to be on friendly terms. Life and death must be seen as a unit, each belonging to the other. If death is treated with respect it is an irrefutable fact that life will be treated likewise. A well adjusted and integrated man or woman will keep the two in balance by allowing one to be a check on the other.

Philip of Macedon had a much healthier attitude toward death than did Epicurus. One of the king's slaves was given a standing order. Every morning he was to enter the king's chambers unannounced. Regardless as to what the king was doing the slave would say in a loud voice, "Philip, remember that you must die!" That was 2,400 hundred years ago, but it refuses to be dated. In the eighteenth century, Jonathan Edwards made 67 resolutions for his own guidance. Number nine reads, "Resolved: to think much, on all occasions, of my own dying, and of the common circumstances which attend death".

Everything that lives must die. Even as the leaves must fall from the trees, so dissolution will come to all things. Man is born to die, therefore, death is as much a part of his human mystery as his life. The Scottish Henry Francis Lyte, an Anglican Evangelical clergyman, portrays this inevitable decay in his immortal hymn. Written on his last Sunday at Brixham following the observance of the Lord's Supper, only a few months before his death in 1847, the words bespeak his awareness of the approaching end.

> Swift to its close ebbs out life's little day;
> Earth's joys grow dim, its glories pass away;
> Change and decay in all around I see:
> O Thou who changest not, abide with me!

We may not like it, but our likes and dislikes have little to do with the realities of human existence. Its origin is not in man. Neither is its termination. Both the beginning and the ending are divine prerogatives and lie totally in the providence of God. Man can do nothing better than to admit and accept this fact as he shapes his days to fit his destiny.

The Countdown Begins at Birth

In a real sense, man begins to die the moment he is born. To be is to begin the progression toward non-being. Our reference is exclusively to physical existence, of course, and has nothing to do with the essential being of man' spirit. Birth is the entrance to a one-way street which leads to a physical dead end. Once it is started the journey must be carried through to completion. The rapidity of travel may be reduced but never stopped. Life moves from the cradle to the grave with uninterrupted continuity. Like a spring of water that breaks through the earth's surface and flows de-liberately into the sea before its flow is stopped, so man moves from his first appearance on the earth to his final disappearance in the ocean of death.

While growing, we are none the less dying. The process of decay is not obvious at first because the innate powers for rebuilding are capable of staying ahead of the gradual deterioration. Not until we approach the early years of middle-age does the deterioration become noticeable as it catches up with the brave bodily efforts to win a losing battle. From there on, it is an escalation of the forces of decay until final dissolution and death terminate the down hill slide. Though the insistent demands of decay can be ignored for a while, they take their toll from the beginning.

The infant is dying as surely as the aged. Twenty-four hours after birth the infant is one day nearer his death than when he drew his first breath. The fires of new life burn vigorously and brightly, but their fuel is being depleted as soon as the flame is sparked. Unquestionably, the most definite thing about birth is its tendency toward death. Man moves from the unconscious darkness of the womb to the utter blackness of the tomb. And the two are related in the fact that birth and death exist for each other, neither being able to exist without the presence of its opposite. If birth is the thesis and death the antithesis, then life is the synthesis. Birth is the genesis of a process for which death is the terminus. The human existence between is the marriage of the two and is held together by the mystically indefinable mucilage called life. As the body deteriorates, it falls apart and the mastic spirit which has held soul and body together is destined to relax its hold as that which is earthy returns to the dust from whence it came.

The bassinet is an archetype of the coffin and the nursery is the gateway to the grave. There is an old riddle about what walks on all fours in the morning, on only two at noon, and on three in the evening. The answer is man who crawls as an infant, walks erect in the prime of his life, and leans on a staff as the years advance. Life is a kind of cyclic affair which begins and ends in instability and helplessness.

Decrepitude Sneaks Up on Us

No one has yet found the secret to perpetual youth. If such a find should ever be made, the discoverer would go to the top of the list of men and women making the most significant contributions to the betterment of human life. Everybody wants to stay young, to postpone the inevitable decrepitude of agedness. Koheleth, the cynic of Ecclesiastes, is dead sure that there is nothing good about the approach of old age. He describes that period of one's life as "evil days" and a time when man must admit, "I have no pleasure in them" (Ecclesiastes 12:1). In fact, his graphic description of the human decline into physical antiquity is unsurpassed by any other literary device. The image of palsy, stooping posture, loss of teeth, dimming vision, poor hearing, bad digestion, early rising, and general debilitation is poetically but accurately depicted. And the wise observer's terse portrayal of final dissolution itself is among the literary world's most beautiful:

> Or ever the silver cord be loosed,
> O the golden bowl be broken,
> Or the pitcher be broken at the fountain,
> Or the wheel broken at the cistern.

The fearful thing about decrepitude is that it sneaks up on us. We begin to grow old long before we are fully conscious of what is happening to us. The slowing up process in early middle-age becomes a joke about which we laugh in order not to be forced to look it straight in the face. But it is not as funny as our jocular attitude would suggest. Growing old can be a beautiful time of life, but it is still rather serious business. Assuredly, it is too sacred a matter for levity of conduct.

If the body is left to its own inclinations, after about 40 years of age, the aging processes are greatly accelerated. For this reason we take greater precautions in the way we live, spend more time with our makeup, and sometimes resort to a younger looking wardrobe. After one has passed the chronological mid point in life, he gets up as tired as when he went to bed. It takes longer in the morning to get started. Walking becomes more of a task and running is out of the question except for the braver ones who have something to prove to themselves. Our houses are built on a one-floor plan so we will not have to climb stairs. Strange pains and unexplainable aches appear. Wrinkles dig their furrows in our faces and the skin on our extremities takes on a dry look. The hair on our heads either loses its color or loosens its roots and clings to the comb. Our entire anatomy takes on a new shape like that of a reversed hour glass and keeping the excess weight off is a daily battle of the bulge. Much of what we used to do and enjoy is now laid aside because we are just too old to act like we once did. The old gray mare is not the only thing that "ain't what she used to be!"

The program chairman of an organization of 35-year-old men invited a well-known after-dinner speaker to address the group at one of its monthly luncheons. With far more insight than he was conscious of displaying, the speaker chose to talk on the theme, "Man Alive, You're Half Dead!" It has been said that life begins at 40. This can be very true for the person who discovers some new motivation for being. But nothing alters the fact that when man reaches this age he is at the mid point of his physical pilgrimage and usually already advanced into the down grade pull.

An Unwise Investment

Every man knows full well that he will not live forever in this world. Yet, in spite of what he knows, he seldom acts upon the basis of his knowledge. To watch him slavishly work to lay in store more than he needs is its own proof of man's false hopes. He invests as though the security of his investments were of an eternal nature. His future is believed to be guaranteed and his peace of mind insured only if enough of this world's goods can be accumulated to offer protection against poverty and want. So man strives, builds, and hoards against the day of his need. In it all, he forgets that the one word which is true and fitting at all times and in all situations is "This too shall pass away".

Did we invest all that we possess in a holding company which is known to be going broke, we would be fools. No one dares to do such a thing. On the contrary, we find the situation which looks most promising for the largest period of time and put our savings into that. The ironic thing about it all is that every last one of these so called sure things is going to go bankrupt. There is not an exception in the whole world. One day the biggest, loudest, and final stock market crash will take place. The heavens themselves will be rolled up as a scroll and "the earth also and the works that are therein shall be burned up" (2 Peter 3:10).

Anyone who allows himself to become totally absorbed by the fascination of this present world has been misguided. He neither perceives who he is nor what the nature of the world is. The things of earth, regarded as ends in themselves, deceive us into assuming that there is nothing beyond which monitors our present use of the world's goods. Man sees himself, in such a misguided philosophy, as a victim of forces that bar him from any kind of continuance after death. There is nothing but this world as we know it, this fleshly existence as we experience it, and the two of us—the world and man himself—have only a brief round in which to enjoy each other. Therefore, man puts everything into the material world with gusto and takes as much as is humanly possible out of it. And in the senseless riot of self seeking, the world is exploited and man is cheated of his human identity and his divine destiny.

The apostolic injunction is quite easily understood if not easily accepted, "The appointed time has grown very short; from now on, let those who have wives live as though they had none, and those who mourn as though they were not mourning, and those who rejoice as though they were not rejoicing, and those who buy as though they had no goods, and those who deal with the world as though they had no dealings with it. For the form of this world is passing away" (1 Corinthians 7:29-31 RSV). These words, in their original Greek, do not mean total separation from everything in the world as though it were evil *per se*. What they do mean is that the Christian must live in a kind of detachment which permits him to use that which God has given in this world without becoming overly dependent on or mastered by it. To use a modern expression, the Christian in his relationship to the world must *hang loose*. For when the consummation of the ages comes, only those who are unattached to the present evil order will survive the judgment which separates the timeless from the eternal.

A Philosophical Optimum

Inevitably, some will react to this entire approach to life under the assumption that living to die stifles and thwarts the growth of healthy specimens of humanity in this world. It is argued that an other-worldly stance will lead to a disregard for the present as if what happens here and now is of no consequence. This is the tenor of the age. Other-worldly is about the worst accusation which can be tacked on to anyone. Thus all but the more saintly among us give a wide berth to persons who talk about life in another world as though it could be as important as the life we now know.

New philosophies and theologies have sprung up in all quarters of both Christian and non-Christian societies. These views of life advocate complete repudiation of the consideration of any real existence outside the interval in man's personal pilgrimage that is bordered by birth and death. Unless he concentrates on the present age alone, man will waste his energies in day dreaming about unrealities while the real life passes him by. What is too often ignored is that the person who has found reality in this world, as it is seen in the wider perspective of the life to come, lives in the most favorable condition for the growth and development of the human organism. That is what we mean by the term *optimum*. C. S. Lewis said it well: "It is since Christians have largely ceased to think of the other world that they have become so ineffective in this. Aim at Heaven and you get earth thrown in: aim at earth and you will get neither." Far from seeing an honest other-worldly philosophy as a deterrent to concern for the betterment of the here and now, such an outlook should be seen as a contributing factor in the best and most lasting investment in the present world order.

If one is desirous of heaven in the world to come, he will be concerned likewise with the coming reign of God on earth. No man who has a legitimate attraction to heaven will be careless about the one place where people are being trained and prepared for that future condition. It will hardly ever be otherwise than that he will dedicate himself to the mission of world redemption in anticipation of the time in the theocracy of God when "the earth shall be full of the knowledge of the Lord as the waters cover the seas" (Isaiah 11:9). And while he is aware that there can be no universal peace until the King comes again to rule in righteousness, the person who prays "Thy kingdom come" (Matthew 6:10) will set himself to the task of helping to create conditions on the earth conducive to beating their "swords into plowshares, and their spears into pruning hooks" (Isaiah 2:4).

Living for the next world does not mean that this one is slighted. Other-worldliness can degenerate into a disinterested attitude about what takes place now. It can console itself with what is to be in some future life and refuse to be disturbed about what is going on in the present. Such a philosophy is in no way related to the dual role played by Christians in the ancient Church. No way of life could have been more oriented to the heavenly world than was early Christianity, yet the present world was tremendously affected by those committed disciples who insisted that death was as important as life. This world became important to them in light of eternity. Without the world to come there would have been little to recommend this one. Earth's training ground took on a new significance precisely because something lay ahead which was directly related to man's stewardship during the allotted period of his earthly sojourn.

Almost everything Jesus says has an eschatological (end of the age) note in it. He seems to have had no hang-ups on which of the two worlds is paramount in man's thinking since they both create a whole picture of life. Our Lord is not so nearsighted that, like some contemporary secularist, He can see nothing but the *secular city*. Neither is He so farsighted that, like some extreme mystic, He can see only *the land far away*. His is 20/20 vision and life is viewed as a whole by Him, not in segments exclusive of each other.

The holiest One who ever lived is the Lord from heaven. Having been in heaven, however, He does not despise this realm of human endeavor. Jesus was very much at home in the world and entered into man's joys (the wedding in Cana) and his sorrows (the many healings and exorcisms). The fact that He knew the bliss of heaven and planned for a return to it was never used as an excuse for being disinterested in this world. We need not fear being criticized for other-worldliness if our dual interests are kept in as proper a balance as were His.

Waiting for The Lord from Heaven

Following His comforting words about the many mansions in the Father's house, our Lord promises that He "will come again" to receive us "that where I am there you may be also" (John 14:1-6). These glorious words are integrally bound up with the second advent. But for those who die before that time, there is also a glad and joyous assurance that the Christian's death is departing to be where He is. In times of persecution, many actually longed for death on the grounds that "to live is Christ, and to die is gain" (Philippians 1:21). Paul himself felt that to be here on the earth is expedient for the cause of Christ, but to be away from bodily existence and with the Lord in heaven is a far superior state. His assurance has been of inestimable comfort to many a dying saint.

Some, in the earliest days of the Christian enterprise, were so sure that Christ was coming immediately that they refused to do any work or make any changes in the status quo. It was not worth it in view of the short time left. All of us know that the one thing they should have been doing, if the Lord were to return immediately, was the giving of every ounce of themselves to the work assigned to them while they waited. One can wait for the Lord without being either lazy or indifferent to what goes on around him.

Whether it is the second coming (which is a certainty) or death (also a certainty as long as the Master tarries) that intrigues us with thoughts of the life to come, we must not stand idly by as though our own personal redemption were all that matters.

A little girl, away from home at camp for the first time, was seen at bedtime with tears on her cheeks. "Are you home sick?" asked the counselor. "No," replied the child, "I'm not home sick; I'm here sick!" Every person, not just the mystic, has this nostalgia for God and the homeland of the soul. But we must neither wring our hands in misery nor flap our wings in ecstasy when, where we are at this moment, needs our best efforts. To be home sick for heaven, and reunion with those we love, is perfectly in order if the lure of heaven does not render us of no earthly account.

As Christ's parable of the pounds points out, the servants of the Lord are to "occupy til [he] come" (Luke 19:13). Each one is to "be about [his] Father's business" (Luke 2:49). If this world were not important, God would never have placed us here. He could have as easily arranged things so that man would be born in heaven without passing through the earth. Since He did not do it that way, it seems clear that He must have more in mind for us while here than a folding of the hands in rest. To *occupy* means more than taking up space, using up air, and fouling up the earth. It means to be involved, to make an investment. But it also means to resist becoming so attached to the earth that we are hesitant to leave it when He comes.

Multitudes of people need the love and concern of the Christian community. Some are sick and cry out for healing; some are hungry and beg for food; some are enslaved and long for freedom. And some are dejected and plead for spiritual fulfillment. Suffering and need should demand our best efforts, especially if we aspire toward life after death. In the first gospel, the beatitudes have a definite future fulfillment in view. Seeing God, being filled with all righteousness, inheriting the earth—these all have an eschatological frame of reference. This is not to say that the rewards cannot begin this very day, but it is to affirm that the future looms large in these sayings. In Luke's shorter account of the Beatitudes, the promises appear to be attainable at once without waiting for the perfected kingdom. There is a wonderful sense in which we can get to heaven before we die. Easily observed in the varied manner in which the beatitudes are presented in Matthew and Luke, is the dual foci which motivated the Son of God—in the world, but not of it; loving the world, yet renouncing it; using the world, but never exploiting it; serving the world, but never mastered by it. Nowhere have the other-worldly and this-worldly concepts been more interrelated and perfectly balanced than in Him who is both Son of God and Son of man.

Taking the Fun Out of Life

No other facet of Christian faith is presumed by the outside world to be as disastrous to personal pleasure and genuine joy as a philosophy which is based on a better life in some distant realm. Karl Marx had this in mind when he called religion "the opiate of the people." A serious dedication to living with a final judgment in one's sights is said to be the one thing which makes one a killjoy. All of us know of persons like that, people so obsessed with judgment day that they make themselves and everybody around them miserable. Life becomes a morose experience built on a foundation of negatives. Indeed, the Pharisees were prime examples of such an unattractive religion.

John the Baptist, preaching the coming of the Messianic kingdom, couched his whole message in dolorous and fearful warnings about judgment. It is impossible to study either his preaching or his life without detecting the strong and fervid denunciations that accompany a prophet committed to a theology of doom. The Baptist was an unhappy man, a killjoy who could not enjoy this world for concentrating on the future. God used him in spite of his lackluster image in the same way that He uses the rest of us. We wonder whether it could have been any other way at this apostate hour in the history of the covenant people.

While some take the fun out of life by thinking only of a future in hell, others accomplish the same by concentrating only on a futuristic heaven. These people, usually good folks, border on the fanatic. At times the border could be described as even worse. The most unfortunate thing in the world is to find believers who live on the lunatic fringe. In such instances, these unseasoned, half turned disciples can radiate no joy in a sinful world. They appear to be completely disinterested in anything except heaven. Their jobs are burdensome, social contacts are frightening, everything is evil, and when they laugh, which is seldom, the sound is nervous and insincere.

All of us have met despondent earthlings on their way to heaven. If anything was felt for them it was pity. Nothing more. One clergyman in particular comes to mind. Seldom ever was he seen to smile. He insisted that the world was so full of sadness he saw little to smile about. And so he added to the far too much misery in the world by contributing his own brand of religious somberness. There is no reason to doubt the sincerity of such Christians or their final acceptance in heaven, but we are not far off base to question their judgment. One wonders how such persons could ever be magnetic enough to take anyone with them. And there is no bigger failure in discipleship than when a poker faced churchman hinders others from entering the kingdom because of his lackluster attitude.

Putting the Fun into Life

Sadness is the devil's religion. The man whose religion makes him miserable either has the wrong kind or he has too much or too little of the right kind. Whichever the case happens to be, he needs a change. John, who gives the most exciting picture of what the world to come is going to be like (Revelation 21-22), also records the words of Jesus in the gospel which bears his name: "These things I have spoken to you, that my joy may be in you, and that your joy may be full" (John 15:11). The joy is a present experience for the Christian who is living now. Simon Peter waxes eloquent in his admonition to the Church to "wait for new heavens and a new earth" (2 Peter 3:13) while at the same time talking about rejoicing with "unutterable and exalted joy" (1 Peter 1:8) right in the present hour. Paul encourages the saints with the promise of being "caught up together . . . in the clouds to meet the Lord in the air; and so we shall always be with the Lord" (1 Thessalonians 4:17 RSV). Yet, in writing to the Galatians, Paul says, "The fruit of the Spirit is love, joy, peace, patience, kindness, goodness, faithfulness, gentleness, self control . . ." (Galatians 5:22). Joy takes a second place to love in the Pauline order of Christian graces only because it is a derivative of it. The book of Acts opens with an angelic assurance of the second coming (quite other-worldly) but the dominant note throughout this history of the ancient Church is joy. In every case, the joy of Christian living in this world was integrally related to the hope of the world to come.

A distinct difference is seen between the somber preacher of doom, John the Baptist, and the bearer of the good tidings, Jesus the Christ. John was the end of an age and Jesus was the beginning of another. And the new age dawned with angels in heavenly chorus and happy worshipers around a humble manger. John was a bit confused by some of the ways of Jesus (Matthew 11:3), and the religious leaders could not understand why He condoned the eating and drinking of His disciples (Luke 5:33-34). A sensitive reading of the Gospels compels us to think of Jesus as a man with much wit and humor. In spite of the seriousness of His mission, He found much to laugh about. It may have been this beautiful blend in His character that drew the disciples to Him.

Jesus made a sizable investment in this world. He gave everything He had, even His life upon a cross, to the recreation of earth into what it had been in the beginning and the reclamation of the divine image in man. Not once did He make that investment, however, with any expectation of a return in this life for Himself. It was all done with an eye to the fulfillment of the kingdom in the coming age. His joyful radiance was based solidly upon the certitude that His mission was of an eternal dimension and could never fail regardless what took place in the interval of His incarnation.

The most radiant and contagious believers are those who dedicate themselves unstintedly to witnessing to the Word of God in life and deed. They love the world because God made it, and they love people because Christ died for them. Untiring in their energies, they pour their life into the service of men in the name of Jesus. In it all, they exude a happy spirit that never turns others away, but draws them to their Lord. Living is fun for these people, because every day is lived in an expectancy of the coming world that demands their best as stewards in this one. Their fun comes from knowing Him who can fling His crown when sinners are redeemed and from being certain that they are continuing the mission of the Son under the guidance of the Spirit. And all of this points to a glorious time of fulfillment and reward, both here and hereafter. Life need not be a vain, meaningless journey with no end in sight. For the Christian it becomes an exciting, purposeful pilgrimage to the Promised Land, each step of the way being an investment in time and eternity.

— Chapter 13 —

Dying to Live

Where Do We Go from Here?

Children have a way of getting keyed up when their parents talk about going someplace. It may be only an outing in the park on a summer day or an evening at grandmother's, but the idea is delightful. And when plans are under way for a vacation in the mountains or at the lake, that is sheer joy to think about. We are all somewhat like little children no matter how old we may be. That we are called children of God is no accident. Though becoming a man should cause one to "put away childish things" (1 Corinthians 13:11), no one grows so old that he cannot get tingly inside at the prospects of a happy adventure in travel.

When the Master discussed His forthcoming journey to the Father's house, the disciples sat rapt in serious attention. Especially did they begin to get nervous with excitement when the Lord stated that His men would someday share in both the journey and the place prepared for them. Like children, whose eyes fill with wonder at the thought of going somewhere they have not been, the disciples were filled with questions and anticipation. So are we beside ourselves today with thrilling emotion when the subject of heaven is mentioned. A kind of homing instinct within is sensitized by the mere mention of the life to come. We are a people going somewhere with joy in our hearts and smiles on our faces.

Since the most primitive times, man has sensed the eternal quality which mysteriously inhabits his human clay. Great care was taken by many of the ancients in preparing for the trip into the next world. Food, horses, chariots, weapons, and servants were buried with them to be used on the long journey. Even the nonbeliever in our Christian faith has an eerie feeling in the presence of death, a feeling that the deceased has really gone somewhere. Different cultures have entertained varied ideas of what happens after death, but they all agree that man does go someplace.

Christians believe there are two places reserved in the next world for men. One is called *hell* and is prepared for the wicked, the unregenerate, the unbeliever. The other is called *heaven* and is prepared for the righteous, the redeemed, the believer. The end justifies the beginning and gives it purpose. Life is a journey traveled on either the high way or the low way, the destination being determined by the way chosen. A Christian is one who has chosen the high way, the path of obedience to Him who has redeemed us with His own blood. He who is in Christ by faith is in a personal relationship with the only Person in history who knew who He was and where He was going both existentially (in this world) and eschatologically (in the world to come).

The older generation has its way of describing this truth in notes of joyful song:

> I am bound for the promised land,
> I am bound for the promised land.
> O, who will come and go with me?
> I am bound for the promised land.

And really, there is little difference in the hope found in young hearts in spite of what has been called the generation gap. In his own way, the modern teenager is saying essentially the same thing:

> I know where I'm going
> And I know who's going with me.
> I know why there's music
> In the quiet summer morning.
> I found a wealth of gold,
> And silver I have plenty.
> I found a light to guide me
> When my way gets dark and stormy.
>
> I'm going where He goes,
> And He'll be there beside me.
> The love for which He died
> Is all I need to guide me.
> I know where I'm going,
> I know where I'm going.
> Where are you going?

Whether it be the joy and hope phrased in the language of an earlier generation or that of the now generation in its blending of the present and the future, there is excitement in the thought of going someplace with Christ.

Adjourned Until

When the moderator strikes his gavel on the podium and says, "This session is now adjourned until two o'clock, at which time we will resume business," everybody knows that nothing has ended. The adjournment is only a temporary break in the proceedings. It changes nothing. At the reconvening of the session, business will be continued as though there had been no interruption. Only one thing is different. The delegates are rested, refreshed, and more relaxed. Death may be thought of as an adjournment between busy sessions of living. It is never termination, only transition. It no more ends anything than taking an afternoon nap concludes a day. Upon awaking, the day's activities are resumed as usual.

No Christian funeral is ever complete until the words of Jesus to Martha are heard again: "I am the resurrection and the life; he who believes in me, though he die, yet shall he live, and whoever lives and believes in me shall never die" (John 11:25-26 RSV). Resurrection is death working backwards. Death for the follower of the Savior is the beginning of a larger life, a life expanded and amplified beyond the narrow confines of earth. In no way does Jesus deny the reality of death, but He does insist that its power is broken and its curse annulled. He who lives and believes in Christ may die physically but he will never experience spiritual death. This explains the contradictory sounding word about dying and living again, yet never dying at all. The fact of the matter is that man dies to live.

So many illustrations can be found by which death is observed in its proper light. To think of it as an adjournment until business is resumed is one way. Another way is to see it as an intermission in a play or a time out in a game. Some like to think of it as a sleep from which the believer awakens in the morning in the Father's house.

In a seven volume set of books called *The Chronicles of Narnia*, C. S. Lewis has written a modern parabolic story of Christian faith and hope for children. The experiences shared by the children in Narnia, a fascinating make-believe world where Aslan (the Lion that represents Christ) guides them through a kind of modern *Pilgrim's Progress,* bring them at last to what is obviously heaven. The closing words of volume seven, *The Last Battle*, are descriptive of what Lewis calls "the real England," while what is presently known of his native country he calls "Shadowlands".

The light ahead was growing stronger. Lucy saw that a great series of many-colored cliffs led up in front of them like a giant's staircase. And then she forgot everything else, because Aslan himself was coming, leaping down from cliff to cliff like a living cataract of power and beauty. . . .

Then Aslan turned to her and said; "You do not look so happy as I mean you to be."

Lucy said, "We're so afraid of being sent away, Aslan. And you have sent us back into our own world so often."

"No fear of that," said Aslan, "Have you not guessed?"

Their hearts leaped and a wild hope rose within them.

"There *was* a real railway accident," said Aslan softly. "Your father and mother and all of you are—as you used to call it in the Shadowlands—dead. The term is over: the holidays have begun. The dream is ended: this is the morning."

And as He spoke He no longer looked to them like a lion; but the things that began to happen after that were so great and beautiful that I cannot write them. And for us this is the end of all the stories, and we can most truly say that all lived happily ever after. But for them it was only the beginning of the real story. All their life in this world and all their adventures in Narnia had only been the cover and the title page: now at last they were beginning Chapter One of the Great Story which no one on earth has read: which goes on forever: in which every chapter is better than the one before.[1]

Perhaps it is helpful to compare death to a hyphen or a comma in the structure of a continuing sentence. All these images are thought provoking, but they have a common weakness. Built into each of them is the acceptance of a pause in time at the moment of physical death. The rhythm of life is not interrupted by anything that happens to the fleshly tenement of man. The person, the essential being in oneness with Christ, lives through the process of physical deterioration and human death.

Benjamin Franklin was right in seeing death as the end of the first chapter. With no break between, the second chapter takes up where the first leaves off. It is the first chapter which determines the direction the plot will take and stimulates either expectancy or hesitation at the prospects of what is to follow. But one's biography must not commence with birth, but with death. All biography must be written in the light of the end of physical existence. The manner of one's death discloses the true nature of his life. Even then, we have only the first chapter. God must gather additional data in the world to come and combine it with the first chapter into a permanent and complete biography of man's life. Inscribed upon the Christian's death certificate and engraved upon his headstone should be the words, "To be continued!"

On April 8, 1945, the cell of Dietrich Bonhoeffer, at Flossenburg, was entered by members of the Gestapo who had come with frightful news. "Prisoner Bonhoeffer," they said, "Get ready to come with us." Those words were recognized by the prisoners as a summons to the scaffold. As his companions bade him goodbye, Bonhoeffer said, "This is the end. For me the beginning of life."

A Going Home at Last

Some speak of death as a returning to our source. This analogy is good if we can avoid seeing in it some carry over from Emerson's transcendentalism or Hindu reincarnation. We are on a non-biblical tangent if we think of death as a merger into the stream of life from whence we came, an absorption into the universal Spirit. No less foreign to the teaching of Christ is the concept of preexistent souls that repetitiously inhabit new forms of human flesh as each preceding one has been discarded. God is our Creator. Therefore, He is our source, and death may be said to be a returning. But, no one except Christ Himself has ever been preexistent. Only He dwelt with the Father prior to His becoming flesh in the womb of Mary. His was a conscious co-sharing of the Godhead. Our being only came about as the Father willed us into existence at human conception. In that sense, and in no other, can we be said to return to our source.

With this point clarified, we may continue without being misunderstood when we speak of death as a going home at last. Men and women in the Judeo-Christian tradition have always thought of themselves as pilgrims in an alien land, sojourners just passing through on their way to heaven. No one has stated this more succinctly than the writer to the Hebrew Christians: "Here we have no lasting city, but we seek the city which is to come" (Hebrews 13:14).

The mournful sounding spiritual also captures the mood of "being away from home" in its opening words:

> I am a poor wayfaring stranger,
> While traveling through this world below;
> There is no sickness, toil, or danger
> In that bright world to which I go.
> I'm going there to meet my father,
> I'm going there no more to roam;
> I am just going over Jordan,
> I am just going over home.

The thought of heaven has always held within it the warmth of homecoming. And there is no joy to compare with that of going back home after years of absence from those we love.

Henry Clay Morrison, founder and first president of Asbury Theological Seminary, had been on an evangelistic tour in England. It so happened that the president of the United States was in Europe at the time and both he and Morrison returned to the States on the same ship. When the ship docked in New York, a great crowd of important people was waiting to welcome the president home. The bands were playing and the people were shouting. Morrison mentioned later to a friend that it was a little disappointing to him to see all those persons waiting to welcome the president home and no one there to welcome him. Whereupon his friend said, "But, Dr. Morrison, you are not home yet!"

We are not home yet as long as we remain in the flesh. Some of us have a long way to go and others of us are nearing the shore. Our years do not always tell us how close or far away we are. But every Christian is on his way. The ship is pointed in the right direction and there must be an opposite shore out there. Someday this ship will open its doors at the gates of home. What a blessed thought that is to one who is buffeted by the storms and threatened by the approach of night. We are going home and Christ Himself is our trusted pilot.

Several years ago a group of us was destined to return from Europe to the States on a partially crippled plane. Though the mechanical problem was supposed to have been repaired during our layover in Shannon, Ireland, there was still a feeling of apprehension. Being scheduled to deplane at Gander, Newfoundland, we were all disappointed to run into severe weather that made it impossible to bring the big plane down. Therefore, we plowed on through the heavy rains and thick haze toward Stephenville, a military airport on the other side of Newfoundland. Obviously, the plane was being flown by instruments, and it appeared that the pilot was experiencing no little difficulty. Needless to say, my brain was host to a thousand unhappy thoughts. We are lost; the airport is not down there; it may be down there but we are going to miss it! Not until the plane was almost on the ground did the runway become visible. Suddenly, it loomed right up in my face and I breathed a sigh of relief. It will be like that someday. After all the fears, disillusionments, and anxieties about death are over, suddenly through the mist the lights will appear on the heavenly runway and we will be home. And all our loved ones will be there to meet us and rejoice in our coming.

Spacious Living

When the signs of decrepitude and decay begin to appear upon the body of a Christian, the world should be able to read the invisible message: *"This tenement being torn down; occupant moving into larger quarters."* The meaning of Jesus' reference to the many mansions is better understood when loosely rendered, "In my Father's house is much elbow room." No one will be cramped in heaven. Our scientists are now telling us that, with the anticipated growth in population, there will soon be standing room only on the earth. When that time comes, if not long before, we can be sure that God will transfer sizeable portions of the earth's people to larger quarters. Maybe over population will only be corrected by the rapture of the saints. The grandest truth of all is that every dying Christian is at once escorted into the spacious and happy world of God and His people.

It is interesting to note that the New Jerusalem, as seen by John (Revelation 21:2,16), covers a land area of two and one quarter million square miles. That is over two-thirds the size of the continental United States. What is even more intriguing is the fact that the City is foursquare (as high as it is wide and deep). When it is observed that Christians in this new dimension will not be restricted to surface living, it is possible that the City itself could house 100 billion people. And we are just talking about the City, the headquarters, from which the redeemed and glorified children of God will have free access to the whole universe. Neither space nor time will hamper the existence of men and women freed from earth's dimensions.

Freedom will be one of heaven's most winsome qualities. Everyone will be totally free to be what he was originally meant to be. No disease to stifle him, no agedness to restrain him, and no more death to cut short what he has begun. Every man will be free to love and serve God with his whole being. With no sin, sorrow, suffering, separation, or any former crippling infirmity, man will be able to spend all eternity exploring the Father's house. The freedom which commences here when we come to know God in Christ will be allowed to blossom into full bloom in the world to come.

A part of the reason heaven will be so spacious is because each person will make room for everyone else. No one there will think first of himself. One reason why there is inadequate space on the earth is because no amount of room is enough when two selfish people are in it. From the peasant's desire to have his neighbor's footage to the king's craving for another's empire, it is one and the same. It is selfishness. Were we to get rid of our selfish ambition for that which belongs to others we would not feel so cramped and afraid. In heaven, of course, there will be no trace of that selfish spirit to infringe on the joys of another. Just the opposite. Finally, each will esteem others better than himself. That is the glory of the place.

The Satisfaction of Fulfillment

Human nature is marked by a dissatisfaction with itself. Inevitably, there is ambition to become more than what one is. In particular, this is true of the Christian who, the closer he lives to the Lord the more he wants to be like Him. The day we arrive in heaven, and not before, that ambition will be satisfied. At that moment, "we shall be like Him" (1 John 3:2). The life of Christ that has begun here with our faith commitment and grown in us through devotion and faithful service will come to full fruition in the next world.

Added to the desire to be like Him who is the perfect Man is the insatiable drive to achieve immortality in one's work. The artist never paints his perfect picture. Even his masterpiece has flaws in his own eyes. No design of the architect is quite right. Something always needs to be bettered. The farmer is proud of the round, red tomatoes he grows, but every harvest brings a determination to improve on last year. Does not every teacher want to be more effective? Does not the preacher feel that each message has been unworthy of the Christ whom he proclaims? Well, heaven is fulfillment. That picture will be painted, that design will come through, that tomato will be grown. Man's deepest desire to achieve in one's work will be satisfied in heaven. There one's work will never be done, but it will be done to satisfaction. It is the frustration that accompanies our labor that tears us apart. In heaven there will be no frustration.

With no sin to render everything touched by man defective, we may expect heaven to provide an atmosphere conducive to uninhibited growth and action. A reasonably good analogy can be found in a garden plot where all parasitic growth has been scientifically removed, the soil has been enriched with only the right nutritive substances, the climate has been precisely controlled, and the seed plants purified of all organic defects. If one can imagine such a perfect place he can begin to perceive something of the possibilities of fulfillment in heaven. Controlled garden plots are an example of the effort to restore nature to its natural state prior to the curse placed upon the ground at the time of Adam's fall. To create such perfect conditions, however, is only temporary and possible within limited areas. Only in heaven will everything be purified and free to develop naturally, everything from the soil to the servant commissioned to live upon it.

The Great Commencement

We began this study on the meaning of life with the presupposition that our earthly existence is a training school. All our years are spent in learning how to live. There are many knocks and bruises involved, but even they have a purpose, when understood, which lends additional meaning to our being here. In fact, everything that happens to us can either be turned into an advantage or a disadvantage depending on our attitude toward life's method of instruction. The whole thing is pointing toward a grand moment of truth.

When a boy or a girl completes the 12-year course of study with successful achievement in each field, the long-awaited day of graduation comes. At times, during the drawn out period of childhood and adolescence, it seems that the end will never come. Often the homework and examinations are so demanding that the growing child wearies of the task. But if he keeps at it, inch by inch, day by day, he finally receives his diploma. And what that diploma means is that now the student is ready to live! He is now prepared to begin. That is why graduation exercises are called commencement.

As odd as it may sound to say so, there is something about a commencement at the close of school that resembles Christian death. All the graduating seniors are choked with mixed feelings. Tears flow freely, even from masculine eyes. Hugs, kisses, and parting words are shared with great emotion. The end has come and severing ties of close friendship is inevitable. Yet, in all the sadness and weeping there is a joy and excitement beyond anything ever before experienced. Somehow the end is not the end. It is rather the beginning, the moment the graduates have awaited for twelve long years. They have worked toward its realization with a sense of awe and anxiety that increases as the time draws near. Leaving the past behind is often hard, but the future is so promising that one has no alternative. And so the end and the beginning are fused into one climacteric moment of nervous anticipation.

At death the Christian is only ready to begin. His whole earthly life has been spent in learning how to fit into the much bigger world reserved for the day when he is prepared to face it. Separation from friends and loved ones is far from easy, but every person is cognizant from a very early time that it must be. A part of the preparation lies in being ready to make the transition as easily and naturally as possible. Having learned his lessons well, the dying Christian is now in a position to commence the life of service that once belonged to man before his sin and has now been restored to him by redemption. Death thus becomes only the cap-and-gown moment when the Lord offers His heartiest congratulations and bids us welcome to the mature world of life.

The mistake which multiplied millions of people insist on making is in looking at fragments as wholes. Man's three-score and ten years are seen as the complete story. His earthly life is not seen as a part of something bigger and larger, but as the larger itself. This interval in time is looked upon as an end rather than as a stage which leads to a beginning. Therefore, man tries to fulfill his total dream by cramming too much, some of which is evil, into his 70 years. He forgets or flatly rejects the possibility of more beyond death. Inevitably, with this kind of philosophy, the whole point of life as a school for training and discipline is ignored. Death is feared, life is wasted, and human destiny is sacrificed. If the divine plan is not to abort before it unfolds in the life to come, man must recognize the purpose of his human pilgrimage and direct his way accordingly.

Paul had the right idea when he wrote to the Christians in Philippi. He clearly stated his own view of life and urged his brethren in Christ to follow his example. With his words we bring our initial question, "What on earth is life all about?" to the only possible answer.

No, dear brothers, I am still not all I should be but I am bringing all my energies to bear on this one thing: Forgetting the past and looking forward to what lies ahead, I strain to reach the end of the race and receive the prize for which God is calling us up to heaven because of what Christ Jesus did for us.

I hope all of you who are mature Christians will see eye-to-eye with me on these things, and if you disagree on some point I believe that God will make it plain to you – if you fully obey the truth you have.

Dear brothers, pattern your lives after mine and notice who else lives up to my example. For I have told you often before, and I say it again now with tears in my eyes, there are many who walk along the Christian road who are really enemies of the cross of Christ. Their future is eternal loss, for their god is their appetite: they are proud of what they should be ashamed of; and all they think about is this life here on earth. But our homeland is in heaven, with our Savior the Lord Jesus Christ; and we are looking forward to His return from there.

When He comes back He will take these dying bodies of ours and change them into glorious bodies like His own, using the same mighty power that He will use to conquer all else everywhere.

Philippians 3:13-21—*The Living Bible*

[1] C. S. Lewis, *The Chronicles of Narnia: The Last Battle* (New York, Harper Collins, 1984) pp.227-228.

To order additional copies of

Getting Ready to Live Forever

Call (800) 917-BOOK

or send $12.95 each + $3.95 S&H to

Books Etc.
P.O. Box 4888
Seattle, WA 98104